CONVERSATION
MARKETING

CONVERSATION MARKETING

How to be Relevant and Engage Your Customer by Speaking Human

KEVIN LUND

This edition first published in 2018 by Career Press,
an imprint of
Red Wheel/Weiser, LLC
With offices at:
65 Parker Street, Suite 7
Newburyport, MA 01950
www.redwheelweiser.com
www.careerpress.com

ISBN: 978-1-63265-138-9
Library of Congress Cataloging-in-Publication Data
available upon request.

Cover design by Joanna Williams
Interior by PerfecType, Nashville, Tennessee
Typeset in New Caledonia LT Std and DIN OT

Printed in Canada
MAR
10 9 8 7 6 5 4 3 2 1

For Huds,
who teaches me more about
how to have a human conversation every day
than I could ever hope to fill in a book.

ACKNOWLEDGMENTS

To my T3AM, for being an incredibly devoted and talented group of people. I'm so grateful to work with you. Thank you. To Stephanie Clark and Dan Rosenberg, for helping me develop the content for this book, and particularly Dan, for allowing me to invade a few Saturday mornings and weeknight evenings.

To Bets. There's no way I could have pulled this off without your undying support and patience, and putting up with my early-morning brainstorms before your first sip of coffee.

Very special thanks to my dear friend and colleague Eileen Sutton, a brilliant story architect, author, and devoted listener. To Raoul Davis, David Novak, and the team at Ascendant Group for making this possible. Another special thanks to Tom Preston ("TP"), a brilliant editor, who's been there since the beginning, and Tom Sosnoff, for single-handedly putting T3 in business. And a shout out to Shannon Vaughn at Aveshka for pitching in at the last minute.

To Joe Pulizzi and the team at Content Marketing Institute for starting the greatest conversation about content marketing ever and perpetuating its explosive growth. To the EO boys in "Forum 5" who know more about me than anyone should. Ever.

To Scotty Lund for always believing in me and literally sharing dreams with me since birth.

To Patrick ("P-Titty,") Tillman, who in every way has been my dearest friend and confidant these past 15 years, and never once doubted my crazy ideas.

And finally, to my boy, Hudson, for enduring many distracted nights with me while I pecked away at a keyboard and heard half of everything you were saying! I love you, buddy.

CONTENTS

FOREWORD

'm an entrepreneur. Launched my first business in
2007. Like most entrepreneurs, I thought we had the
best product in the industry. All we had to do was build
awareness and it would sell like hotcakes.

Until it didn't.

In hindsight, the product was fine . . . but all our conversations revolved around our "amazing" product. We
were cold-calling and cold-emailing, hitting the trade
shows, aggressively pitching the features and benefits.

It was incredibly challenging . . . and painful.

Two years later, we (finally) realized our problem.
We were trying to extract value from a group of buyers
(audience) before delivering any value to them. We were
trying to start conversations with people who didn't
want (at all) to talk with us.

What if we could switch the model? What if we
delivered amazing value to our audience without asking
them to buy? What if we listened to our audience, found

out their deepest and darkest problems, and delivered value outside of our products and services?

What started with instructional articles led to a magazine, an event, a podcast, and a suite of other "information-first" products that focused squarely on providing the best content to that audience that you could find anywhere in the world.

Slowly, over time, the conversations started. The audience began to reach out to us. They actually wanted to talk with us now. We were providing so much value to them. Through calls, emails, tweets . . . every day there were more people reaching out than the previous day.

Then, they started to buy the things we offered, and asked us to launch products we didn't have. And what started as an incredible failure in 2007, became the fastest-growing company in our industry just five years later. I almost gave up, but luckily learned my lesson in time and created an amazingly successful company.

Are you in a similar situation? Is your marketing broken? Are you always pitching products instead of listening and taking orders? Is your marketing just another expense, or is it a game-changer?

Kevin and I had the privilege of meeting and working together in 2009, just as I was changing course. At that time, Kevin was making his own waves helping financial firms dig themselves out of the "Great Recession" by developing content marketing strategies with phenomenal results. After taking a closer look at what he was doing, it didn't take long for me to realize he, too, was onto something unique.

This book will teach you the small tactical and big strategic thinking to change the way you communicate with your customers. Communication professionals who take Kevin's advice to heart will see an amazing transformation in your business . . . that your customers will actually *want* to talk with you.

My wish for you, before you engage in this book, is to be open to this change. For the next 200+ pages, put aside what you think marketing and sales is, and be open to what marketing and sales should be.

—Joe Pulizzi
Founder, Content Marketing Institute, and author of five best-selling marketing books including *Killing Marketing* and *Content Inc.*

INTRODUCTION

*H*ow can I help you?"
Five simple words to start a conversation. There are many ways to say them. But who is saying them and how the words are said can make all the difference. Whether they're words used by a gum-chomping teenager serving you at a fast-food counter or a suit-and-tie professional you meet at a networking event, one may be obligatory whereas the other is more genuine. But there's more.

At a minimum, all relationships begin with a "handshake moment"—those first few seconds that say a great deal about the character of the person standing before you. Why should a company be any different? "Content marketing" has evolved traditional marketing into a new level of personalization as a means of bridging the gap between the old guard (TV, radio, and print) and the new (digital and social media).

And though content marketing has become big business, it remains largely misunderstood as a legitimate means of starting or growing your business. Budgets can be big, or next to nothing, depending upon whom you're trying to communicate with and what you're trying to accomplish.

Gone are the days of blasting your message to unwitting consumers. They want to trust who they turn to for their information needs. They expect transparency. With the clamor of choices fighting for their attention, what makes your message stand apart from the crowd?

Content marketing, when done right, builds long-term relationships and drives meaningful action through conversation with your audience. Websites, videos, social media, magazines—you name it. It provides people with information that is valuable and relevant while it positions you as a trusted resource. It attracts customers, and it retains them.

What Is "Content," Really?

For all the talk about content, there are a surprising number of people who still don't know how to describe it. This is the best definition I've heard: *"A fancy piece of terminology for movies, television, plays, videogames, books, magazines, any form of news, information, or entertainment that people consume with any of their sensory organs other than their taste buds. Soup, for example, is not content. But a video of soup is."*[1]

Too many companies continually produce content for content's sake. They open a Twitter account, start a Facebook page, write a blog, start curating content, or post mindless copy. It's not a positive strategy. Instead, they need a set of rules to guide them in engaging their audience in today's demanding world. Audiences aren't tolerating rote copy or robotic, frivolous content anymore. Branded content, in particular, should be outward facing, not inward focused, in a human, relevant, and useful way.

Unless content is part of a conversation—a meaningful, two-way dialogue between you and someone else—it's just part of the online noise. Content, when used as a marketing tool, along the path to purchase, should first serve the information needs of your customer, not your own. Content without context is useless. And most often, that context is found through conversation.

Conversation Is King

How does conversation fit in here, and how do we define it? Some might define it as an exchange of opinions and ideas. Others might see it as swapping rhetoric. The dictionary defines it as a spontaneous interactive communication between two or more people that involves a verbal exchange. But did you ever contemplate the relevance of conversation in a business marketing setting? It can be quite different.

In a business marketing setting, effective conversation elevates content from a tired commodity to prose that motivates. It "humanizes" a brand. But inserting exclamation marks in your copy to feign emotion and hiding behind the language of "you" aren't enough. The secret sauce of content marketing isn't channel distribution, customer engagement, or key performance indicators. It's much simpler. It's how you speak with your audience—not only *what* you say, but *how* you say it. If content is the what, conversation is the how.

Picture this. The average person in the U.S. is exposed daily to a sea of more than 3,000 marketing messages.[2] But is it the start of a conversation? Hardly. In most cases, it's simply noise to be tuned out by the majority of the crowd.

How will you rise above the noise? What will make your brand stand out and seem particularly interesting to a target audience? Oftentimes, the differentiator is kick-ass content, and whether it's engaging and memorable enough to compel your audience to choose whether to do something meaningful, stick around for more, or forget about it ten seconds after they see it. The trick to delivering the right kind of content to the right audience at the right time is a deeper understanding of who they are, what they want to talk about, and how they want to be spoken to. At the heart of this is "conversation marketing"—the intersection of one-to-one conversation and content marketing.

This book applies some tactical rules for having a conversation within the context of your content marketing strategy. In life, wars are not won on strategy alone, but the sound tactics in approaching each battle. Tactics are critical to the success of a campaign. And simple conversation tactics are the "missing links" in many failed content marketing campaigns that would otherwise be successful.

This book brings marketers and businesses closer to how to create the personal connection critical in a content marketing strategy. Although most companies know they need to invest in content, many are struggling with doing it effectively.

Content marketing today is so much more than it was in the early days when John Deere created *Furrow Magazine* in 1895 to educate farmers. Today's content marketing is about stimulating an audience with useful information they need to know, in an unobtrusive way, and nudging them to do something—to take action, to get involved, to join a movement, or to purchase a product.

For those who think you have to choose between content and traditional marketing, understand that content marketing plugs into and complements an existing overarching marketing strategy. It's no longer separate but equal. Content marketing is one of the fastest-growing segments in marketing because of the sheer volume of content being produced. By 2019, content marketing is projected to be a $300 billion industry, with marketers increasing their content marketing spend 75 percent in 2018.[3]

Where Conversation and Opportunity Met

I got into this business because I was passionate about helping small investors learn how to navigate the financial markets more easily and safely—through eye-level education. The "tech crash" of 2000 rendered a lot of innocent folks broke, scared, and mistrusting of the financial markets. The trading magazines I read were intimidatingly complex and full of jargon, and the investing magazines, which were mostly for the "buy and hold" crowd, felt stodgy and outdated. I knew if I could distill the complexities of active investing into a fun conversation that anyone could understand and actually enjoy, they would trust the markets again, and feel more confident and empowered to take matters into their own hands. If they felt more confident, they would make better decisions, invest smarter, and improve their lives.

A few years later, literally on the back of a cocktail napkin, I sketched out an idea allowing me to scale this belief to a large audience by having a conversation with them through the lens of content marketing. As an investing instructor at the time, something I uniquely understood to be the missing link between the companies that produced financial services products and the investors who used them was simply having the right conversation. The goal, then, was simply to put the information needs of investors first, keep it light, don't pitch, and the product will sell itself.

In 2007, just as the original iPhone was making its debut and smartphones were about to change the way we would all communicate with one another, I pitched an idea to an online brokerage firm that they should consider engaging in a different kind of conversation with their audience that nobody else was having yet: a print magazine that focused solely on trading strategies in a plain-English, humorous, and irreverent way. They loved the idea, and the conversation that took shape was *thinkMoney*, published quarterly, focusing squarely on active trading strategies, tools, tips, and the goings-on in the trading industry. My firm, T3 Custom, was in business, and what might have looked like unfortunate timing in 2007—as the planet was about to simultaneously collapse economically and go all digital—ended up being serendipitous. Despite the headwinds, *thinkMoney* was exactly the smart, reassuring offline voice that was needed at a time when there was so much distrust with any brand connected to Wall Street. After TD Ameritrade purchased our client in 2009, they went all in on *thinkMoney*, and it went on to become one of the largest circulated magazines of its kind in the world, with thousands of loyal fans, some of who admitted to waiting by their mailboxes for the next issue to arrive!

That kind of loyalty isn't earned because of drab content that anyone can write. It came from a thoughtful, conversational approach that honored the audience's time, focused on their interests, filled their knowledge gaps, and gave them aspirational content to get them to do something meaningful for themselves and, ultimately, the bottom line of the brand.

In the beginning, we weren't afraid of the fact that a magazine like this hadn't been done before, and there was no data point that could tell us it would succeed, other than simply knowing our audience very, very well. And that's the point. A good idea that can't be validated because it lacks historical comparisons doesn't make it a bad strategy or risky. Brands like Red Bull, Marriott, and American Express, which we'll discuss later in the book, knew this all too well also, and have had tremendous success creating content brands that broke all the rules.

Welcome to the Conversation Age

The Stone Age overhauled how early humans worked with the advent of tools. The Agricultural Age revolutionized human beings' use of land. The Industrial Age transformed humans' work with the dawn of machines. The Information Age enriched human knowledge and communication via electronic media.

The Conversation Age, likewise, finds us in the midst of another evolutionary process. During the 1990s—the heyday of the Information Age—a new form of persuasion architecture emerged. Email and the Internet became incredibly efficient pipelines for new business, forever changing the way we bought and sold products and services. Banner ads and email campaigns were like the land grabs of the Wild West. It was all an unexplored frontier. When the Internet reached critical mass in the 1990s, the paradigm was simple: Get eyeballs. Throw a bunch of ads on anything with a dot-com, and a relatively predictable number of those eyeballs would convert to customers. The more eyeballs, the more companies would spend on ads to be on your site. It was so novel and exciting, consumers didn't think too much about what companies had to say. They were having too much fun clicking buttons! And companies weren't too concerned about personalizing their messaging beyond slogans and taglines. They sold products. Anything that didn't immediately translate into sales was a waste of time.

The landscape rapidly changed, however, after the technology industry "crashed" in the early 2000s. Today, differentiation is critical if brands want to compete. And it often comes down to content. Learning to use conversational techniques through a content marketing lens to touch the hearts and minds of customers should be a top priority for today's marketers in every field. It's no longer effective to merely shout at consumers through one-way megaphones like television, radio, print, and banner ads. Instead, today's more sophisticated consumers demand transparent, honest, and authentic dialogue.

Social media has afforded brands the ability to engage in a transactional dialogue, giving them a bigger platform and louder voice. This new power has forced the modern brand to be completely transparent, and in many cases, more vulnerable in its storytelling. Thus, the Conversation Age requires businesses to educate, motivate, inspire, and even entertain their customers, all while telling a human "story." When brands speak human, this conversation begins and the journey from customer discovery to customer loyalty can begin.

The implication in this era of conversation, then, is your need to have healthy engagement with customers that not only defines your brand's personality but also enhances its credibility and reputation in their minds. In other words, one of the key factors distinguishing you from your competition in the marketplace is sounding less like a marketer and more like a peer—hence, "speaking human." And although you might think otherwise, your brand personality is not limited to catchy slogans, slick logos, and eye-popping website designs.

Content that conveys your brand's voice and character can share equal footing with traditional marketing techniques, and work together to express your brand personality and make your relationships with your customers worthwhile and memorable. It's all about connecting with the world and its varied cultures in a way that they're able to connect with you in return. Find the common emotional hot button for your audience, and indelibly insert your brand's mark into your customers' hearts and minds so they think of you first when they need you—even if you're just selling gum.

Consider "The Story of Sarah and Juan," a 2015 ad for Extra gum with a cover version of "Can't Help Falling in Love" performed by Hailey Reinhart. The simple love story of Sarah and Juan begins in the hallway of high school, where Juan helps Sarah with her dropped papers and she thanks him with a stick of gum (Extra, of course). Later the love story takes audiences through the seasons, from high school to college to career, with kisses and Extra. Audiences get glimpses of Juan drawing on the wrappers. The climax of the story is an art gallery showing of Juan's Extra wrapper art of their chronological love story, which ends with a drawing of Juan proposing to Sarah. When she turns, Juan is on his knees proposing to her as the song ends.

Here are the first-week statistics for Extra's sweet love story set to music (before it ever made its primetime television debut):

- 7 million YouTube views.
- 78 million Facebook views.
- 1.1 million Facebook shares.
- 19K downloads of "Can't Help Falling in Love" performed by Hailey Reinhart.[4]

So how did a gum company achieve this? It's simple: They chose emotional storytelling with values and vision (gum is a part of our lives), rather than a rote commercial touting features and benefits (our gum is the most spear-minty and lasts the longest). Instead of pitching well-written sales jargon and talking about how great your products/services are, offer your audience a front-row seat to your story. Simply put, don't just sell me gum. Give me an experience to remember.

Conversation Marketing at Its Core

For decades, traditional marketing and advertising tactics that detached the brand/customer relationship dominated the media. Today, your audience demands more authenticity and relationship with your brand. Like billboards on a highway, traditional marketing is largely based on one-way communication where there is little to no opportunity for customers to respond and communicate their reactions in real time. Without a response from your customers regarding what they actually expect from you, it's difficult to make relevant changes to sync with their likes and dislikes. It's largely a game of shoot first and ask questions later.

Conversely, as an astute content marketer who "listens" to your audience and anticipates what they need, you'll develop a brand personality that is relatable. This gives you license to engage in a healthy two-way exchange of information driven by the rules set by your customers, not by you.

And the missing link needed in the large number of botched content marketing campaigns (particularly in social media) is conversation. But you have a blog, you say. That's a good start. But you've only just begun.

The Bottom Line

It's important to understand your audience and how to talk to them in their language. When you earn their trust, you can then prove your credibility by delivering novel ideas, not run-of-the-mill sales copy. Conversation replaces the one-way dialogue of bullhorn marketing with a two-way process encouraging inquiry and feedback to let you know what's on your customer's mind.

To start, ask yourself, "How can we speak to our audience? What do we want them to do? What are we offering them that they can get nowhere else?" When you ask these questions, you begin the process of customer engagement according to the new rules of marketing. And that puts you on the path of developing customer affinity and, ultimately, customer loyalty to your brand.

Given the fact Americans now spend more than ten hours per day on "screen time,"[5] it's often easier to reach a larger customer base through digital channels like social media. As a result, when you post an advertising campaign on Twitter or Facebook, it could be viewed by an enormous number of audiences, and it will also allow you to monitor your performance by analyzing consumer responses and behaviors in real time.

By keeping tabs on your audience's likes, shares, and click-throughs, tracking consumer patterns in real time has never been easier. Additionally, making adjustments to your campaign to ensure better performance is equally performed with ease. Once you receive a collective response to your marketing message from your audience, the conversation has begun. With this open line to your audience, the goal is to keep the conversation going so these acquaintances turn into loyal friendships.

Content Marketing in the Conversation Age

Although the power of great-quality content cannot be denied, it's fast becoming commoditized. Today, content is everywhere, and we've become increasingly focused on creating "content" for content's sake—often technical and terribly sterile—rather than taking care to make the content warm and humane. Conversation marketing cuts through industry jargon and sterility by capturing customers' emotions with the goal of elevating them to your frequency. This notion is critical for the conversation to become immersive.

. . . .

Prudential: A Case Study

Financial giant Prudential came out with an advertising campaign representing conversation marketing at its finest. Financial planning is a complicated and often frightening prospect for most people. This is the reason it was essential for Prudential to adopt the conversation marketing approach and build enough credibility, so their customers trusted the brand with their hard-earned retirement money.

The company created a series of videos advertising their "Bring Your Challenges" campaign.[6] By means of this campaign, Prudential urged people to share their opinions about how much money they thought they needed to retire and lead a financially secure life. In order to make their retirement planning easier for the customers, Prudential simply asked them, "What if you live to be ninety?" and urged them to plan for a long retirement. The theme of their campaign was "Together we can create retirement income that lasts."

Ultimately, Prudential got everyday folks thinking about and addressing the situation in a more conversational manner. Complete with simple arguments and thoughtful before-and-after imagery, the brand put forth a marketing campaign that not only engaged their target audience, but also helped them understand Prudential's services. And they achieved this by calling upon the assistance of the very audience they were addressing.

A worthwhile conversation does not provide a fixed explanation or interpretation of a story. Instead, it leaves the audience with room for making their own interpretations according to their understanding of the message. You'll likely agree the most memorable experiences in anyone's life are those that triggered some sort of emotional reaction. The Prudential advertising campaigns featured conversations triggering a series of emotions ranging from hope, humor, surprise, and even fear, and creates a lasting memory in the audience's mind.

. . . .

Conversation Marketing Concepts to Think About

Though it's hard for companies focused on "being the best" to imagine, one of the most effective approaches in securing your place within your customer's hearts is displaying your vulnerability and showing your brand is human, too. Remember: Regardless of how well established your brand might be, there will always be people who will be meeting you for the first time. Proceed thoughtfully.

Gone are the days when consumers graded brands based on their market position. People today appreciate honesty and humility over "corporate speak" and are far more responsive to personalized conversations that serve to make them feel connected to you—that you're one of them. You must be more approachable and welcoming rather than the other way around. You must come to the market exceeding consumer expectations and providing them with tailor-made solutions to their specific problems—always working toward meeting or exceeding their needs. Generalization is one of the biggest turnoffs for today's discerning consumer. You must engage with your clients, current and potential, and highlight the product or service you're offering in a way that's specifically designed to fulfill their individual needs.

So, how exactly does a conversation marketing approach add value to your business?

1. It promotes engagement. Companies that are only interested in delivering one-way information to a target set of customers without attempting to get to know them will lose in the Conversation Age. Just like with personal relationships, if your message is all about you and how great you are, people will start to avoid you. Conversation takes you from robotic and boring to likeable and human, making it easier for you to connect with your consumers on a deeper level.

It fosters their affinity to your brand, and consequently, makes your products more appealing.

2. It adds a personal touch. Making your customer feel valued is a critical aspect of effective marketing. Through conversation, you get to know the likes and dislikes of your customers and offer them personalized solutions to suit their specific needs. When you engage with your customers on a one-to-one level and customize your message and story to their varied needs and requirements, you make them feel special and appreciated.

3. It maximizes conversions. Conversation lets you develop a lasting connection with your potential customers and ensures that they respond positively to your product or service. When customers trust a brand, they will automatically gravitate toward that company without giving it a second thought.

Unlike the ages that preceded us, the Conversation Age is about human evolution at a cerebral level. Though there's no single tactile invention to point to in this age that makes life better, more efficient, or goods and services, such as the plough, the assembly line, or the personal computer, we are reinventing how we speak to one another in ways that influence behavior like no time before this. And it's beginning to look remarkably like a Darwinian theory unfolding before us.

Based on his theory of natural selection, Charles Darwin hypothesized that giraffes once had shorter necks. Eventually, as other, more dominant herbivore species competed for food sources low to the ground, some giraffes with unusually longer necks were able to feast on food just out of reach of the other animals. Dumb luck for the short-necked giraffes became good fortune for their long-necked brethren. The long-neckers that survived paid their genes forward and proliferated, and eventually all giraffes had long necks.

Now, though the short-necked giraffe may have been an unwitting victim of the evolution of their species, today's businesses can choose their fate. Today's consumer is smarter, more informed, and less trusting than consumers of past generations. Choose the short neck and ignore content marketing at your peril, or choose the long neck by embracing it and not only survive, but thrive. Brands that ignore the principles of conversation in their content marketing program are tacitly choosing competitive disadvantage over opportunity. Just as fair pricing, great service, and reliable technology are basic attributes of a successful business model, human, conversational content is essential for survival.

To sum up, instead of sticking with the age-old business-to-business (B2B) or business-to-consumer (B2C) marketing concepts, as a conversation marketer, you must strive to create an H2H, or human-to-human, strategy. With humility and a little story, educate your customers on the impact of your products and services, not on feature sets or attributes. When done correctly, you develop a trust with your customer base that makes it nearly impossible for others failing to do so to compete. Trust is the foundation and mortar that builds and sells a brand. Ultimately, authenticity in the words you say drives the kind of trust and value, when engaged, loyal customers can provide. And it all begins with gaining the attention of your audience.

The Content Struggle

As businesses are clamoring to jump on the content marketing bandwagon, content itself is becoming increasingly commoditized, and many companies are losing sight of the quality of the conversation they're supposed to be having with their audience. These businesses are simply checking off the boxes on their content marketing checklist without much thought to formalizing an effective and meaningful strategy that helps their customers. As a result, there's a glut of blah content out there, seemingly created in a vacuum, and the data emerging from within the same vacuum is providing inconclusive results and "false positives." In other words, it might be working for search engines, but it's not working for humans who actually read the content.

That is where this book comes in. *Conversation Marketing* is a how-to guide that takes you through ten key principles on how to engage in a conversation with your customers—within your content marketing program—that's meaningful, relevant, and trusted, and that ultimately drives them to engage with your brand. By applying these principles, you should be able to successfully strengthen your customer conversations and amplify your content marketing results.

Let's Delve In

The following pages will explore in depth the Conversation Age that we find ourselves in and the ten key principles of conversation marketing. These principles are designed to help businesses go from yawn to yay through evolved content marketing concepts that work. The topics we'll explore are:

- How to earn attention.
- How to tell a story.
- Being humble.
- Where to have the conversation.
- Opening up and listening.
- Being relevant (on a molecular level).
- How to start a conversation.
- Knowing when to stop talking.
- Getting your customer involved.
- Ditching the checklist.

Conversation marketing is an engaged process of knowing your audience, understanding their pain points, and motivating them to do something beyond watching thirty-second commercials and being shouted at. *Conversation Marketing* is the nuts and bolts of how to have a conversation within your content marketing strategy.

PART ONE
PLANNING

"Think before you speak" is usually good advice. Before you have a conversation with your audience, take the time to think about how you want to come across and how you plan to make a difference in the lives of the people you're talking to. Whether it's 100 people or 1,000,000, this is your handshake moment with each person. What are you going to do with it?

CHAPTER 1

Earn Attention

*B*lah blah blah. . . .
That's the sound most consumers hear when companies market their products. Today, consumers expect—no, demand—more from businesses than mere slogans and stale advertising campaigns. Even so, most companies struggle to effectively communicate even the most essential messages in order to differentiate their brand in a crowded, confusing marketplace.

How Do You Earn Attention?

The easy answer is to do the opposite of what most everyone else is doing. That means don't deliver clichéd, boring content, written only for robots (search engines). It's unsustainable for you and your brand as well as frustratingly futile for the audience you're trying to reach.

The answer is to speak human, engaging your audience, gaining their attention, and setting your brand apart.

Take off your own marketing hat for a moment. As modern consumers, we've begun to turn a deaf ear to traditional advertising messages, which continue to inundate our mailboxes and in-boxes, and interrupt our favorite radio and TV shows. In the same way, we've revolted against digital "spam" by installing ad and popup blocking apps, registering our cell phones on the do-not-call list, "cutting the cable," and using other uncluttering technologies to rid our days of unwanted advertising messages.

In the wake of this consumer rebellion, companies are left scrambling for effective solutions, ultimately turning to content marketing to help them make and maintain meaningful connections with their customers. However, like many marketing innovations incubated to solve problems, content marketing is at risk of quickly losing its poignancy and purpose in both application and adoption.

Early adopters of content marketing understood it as a disciplined approach to communicating with target audiences. Fast and fair-weather "followers" considered the content marketing methodology a fresh, new, clever term for the old approach of traditional, one-way "broadcast" media that simply used "more words." Not only have they missed the point of the innovation, they have also completely missed the opportunity to tell a simple, human story intended to educate, inform, and even entertain customers.

The result: These marketers fail to fully capture mind—and market—share because their message neither resonates, nor "sticks" with existing or emerging customers. And so, the time has come for brands to move beyond "content" for content's sake and toward a deeper level of engagement through "conversation," not just swaths of more content.

Differentiation Is Key

There are two ways to differentiate yourself from the failing marketers—with the words you say and how you say them. The words and visuals you choose to create your content, when combined with your well-thought-out brand personality, will have a monumental impact on the success of your content marketing strategy. Together they work to create a memorable experience for your customers.

How? By going a step beyond the nuts and bolts of content marketing and embracing the need to create a heart-felt, real, two-way interaction in which both parties are invested. It's time to return to a time when selling was done among friends, neighbors, community, and family members. They weren't considered "audiences" then, but instead, a diner whose order the waitress knew by heart or a customer whom the barber knew wanted "a little off the sides and a fresh shave" before they sat in the chair. These were the days when "marketers" were part of customers, everyday lives, when they knew the audience as "individuals."

It's the original premise behind content marketing—in which 26 percent of today's annual marketing budgets are being spent to educate an audience rather than sell them.[1] The conundrum is this approach falls short in connecting with consumers and creating a one-on-one dialogue, becoming a traffic-driver rather than a true marketing device. Today, companies need to re-imagine their approach in a way that earns their customers' attention and makes a real connection.

How? By communicating conversationally rather than talking at them like a politician giving a speech. You know it as a conversation—an immersive, two-way communication involving a healthy exchange of information. In content marketing, information delivered through conversation equals success.

We're all aware a business is largely driven by its customers and flourishes only when the brand can deliver what is promised. Consumers are bombarded with a wide range of options from which to choose. And because the average person already sees 3,000 messages every day from well-established brands, it's essential your shout-out is relevant, engaging, and memorable.[2]

Your Handshake Moment

The first part of a new conversation between two people typically involves the handshake. A "handshake moment" in conversation marketing kicks off a new relationship between a brand and a prospect or customer.

Consider your company's story and the way your company should introduce itself to the world. Are you only selling a product or service, or are you making a difference in peoples' lives? Ask yourself what your company is passionate about. Now, ask your colleagues what they believe your company is passionate about. It's not products and services. You aren't passionate about a product or service; you're passionate about what your product or service will do to make the lives of your customers better. The most successful companies aren't successful because they spout their attributes—as business thought leader Simon Sinek states in his well-known TED talk: "It's not about the what [i.e., what you do], it's about the why [i.e., why you do it]."[3]

In essence, it's a return to speaking human. The seemingly lost art from a time when a handshake meant something—a real, defining moment of human experience backed up by honesty, trust, and performance. Specifically, this simple philosophy provides the road map to achieving the coveted handshake moment, one that a company can have with the person on the other side of the screen to start a relationship and is built primarily by trust and performance.

Every handshake moment is a touch point with your brand that says, "Hey, nice to meet you" or, in the case of existing customers, "Welcome back. I've got something I want to share with you." During these moments, your audience should feel as if you're talking to them as an individual, not a cog, in every piece of content you put out there. You never know when someone is going to stumble onto you for the first time, so it's a good idea to think of each piece of content as a way to make a good impression.

Up until now, businesses have struggled with linear, low-level, or one-way communication. It's a purely human phenomenon at the core of every conflict or stalemate, from the ones experienced at home, at work, and in communities. In the focus on transmitting information, human beings often lose sight of the critical need for feedback, response, and an actual "human" exchange of emotions or ideas.

Today's social networking channels may superficially reach customers with results while in reality they are often only perpetuating linear, low-level communication. For example, say you're on Twitter and Facebook and you're tweeting and posting five times a day, apparently growing your fan and follower base like clockwork with your strategic ad buy. Even so, your zealous, disciplined approach doesn't mean you're actually doing so *effectively*. Who, exactly, are all those followers, friends, and fans? Are you really speaking human, developing a connection, or telling an authentic story? Or are you simply tweeting and posting just to check it off your task list, and your followers are re-tweeting or "liking" you for the exact same reason? If that's the case, then they're not really followers—and they're far from friends!

Speaking human is more than opening a communication channel for the channel's sake or using social media because someone at a seminar told you that you should. The all-important handshake moment is where people get a glimpse of the real you for the first time, and because that is the case, what do they find? Will they be greeted by a jargon-filled sales pitch? A catchy slogan? A classic press or media kit? Or, instead, will they find a genuine person, someone they might want to reach out to and shake hands with in real life? If you're not asking these questions, let alone answering them satisfactorily, chances are your content is simply traditional advertising disguised as "substance" wearing a new suit.

Social media etiquette insists we do not *sell* ourselves but, rather, *share* ourselves. We must learn to read the signals telling us when to drop the jargon, cut the BS, and instead talk, authentically and truthfully, to those we *hope* might buy our product or service. Yes, we sell things, and so we must provide essential information about policies, performance, and the like, but good content marketing is also about providing information and education. We shouldn't have to sell ourselves.

Finding Your Brand Personality

It's easy for people to know *what* you do. But do they know *who* you are? People typically size each other up within the first few seconds of meeting. They ask, "Can I trust this person?" and "Do I relate to them?" While doing so, they look for visual and audible cues—how others are dressed, their body language, what they say and how they say it—all with the goal of making a connection. It's in this moment that you have the opportunity to begin to share your brand voice.

In conversation marketing, your company's "voice" and "tone" shoulder the burden of answering potential customers' questions:

"Who are you?"

"Can you be trusted?"

"Can I relate to you?"

Your Voice

This is your brand's content personality and style, like a signature look for a car manufacturer or a fashion designer. If you're into those things, you just know the difference between a Porsche and a Honda, or a Coach handbag from a Louis Vuitton. Your choice of words and how you use them will dictate whether the prospective customer reading or hearing them will connect with you and your brand because you stand out.

Forget about what they need from you. First, they need to *like* you. The goal of creating the right voice is to connect with them by speaking in colorful, yet plain English, and getting them to act *right now*. To do so, you may have to step out of the corporate conventional wisdom vortex and speak in a voice that is more cocktail conversation than boardroom meeting.

Today's consumer is not looking for the voice of an Oxford professor. They're looking for a personality they can relate to, a voice that's familiar—"one of us." Someone with whom they can really connect. For new clients, your first tweet could become your handshake moment. Each tweet, Facebook entry, and blog post should be crafted with a human voice, not a robotic one.

Your Tone

Once you determine your brand voice, you must establish your brand's tone, also called the tone of voice in some circles. If voice is your content personality and style, tone is your attitude. A designer's style is her voice, her fall line is her tone. Typically, the tone of social media is peer-to-peer; after all, you're talking to a friend. It's warm, fun, interesting, and inspiring. Avoid talking down to your audience. And dump the bank-speak. Everything should be as clear as if you were talking to a friend—comfortable, interesting, engaging. We listen to our friends, but we mute the commercials.

Whether you're utilizing social media or the web, people are looking for solutions to problems, cures for pain points, and, on some level, entertainment. Most new clients are not looking to be entertained by you (yet), so they should be greeted with a genuine human touch that is peer-to-peer, not teacher/student, not coach/player, and not advisor/client.

Avoid dry and boring speech and deliver your message in a new and unique way. You want to present fresh messages they can't get anywhere else and *they* want to share. Your tone should reflect your brand voice. The following "Four Cs" are good high-level rules of thumb to use when designing your tone.

The Four Cs

- Clear: Use plain, understandable language.
- Clever: Be memorable, amusing, heartfelt, and captivating. Clever isn't about humor. Instead, clever means consolidating your complex messages into "edible" content your readers will devour and share. Without cleverness, your post will be quickly forgotten.
- Concise: Lean the copy. Say in five words what you want to say in ten. Cut, then cut again.
- Consistent: Your voice and tone don't have to be the same for every audience, but it should be consistent for a particular audience, across all your channels. After all, you're not going to try to speak the same language to an aging baby boomer as you would a teenager.

Once you understand the Four Cs relevant to all content, you'll want to color the tone to your target audience specifically. For example, here's how a company might color a tone targeting millennials on Twitter.

- Smart: Not engineer smart. Authoritative and trustworthy.
- Edgy: Slightly unconventional, always tactful—avoid sex or politics.

- Witty: Clever, but not sophomoric. Think Trevor Noah, without the politics.
- Approachable: Inviting and irresistible, not intimidating.

So, What About the Content?

Now that you've figured out your personality, let's talk content. As you're planning your content strategy, consider a few things. Content that's obvious is a straight line to boring and unmemorable. Find the right angles, and don't be afraid to challenge conventional wisdom. If you're trying to engage your audience, they're craving something that can be heard above those 3,000 other daily messages you're competing against. You'll have a tough time achieving this if you only write for robots. If your content sucks, it won't matter if you're on page one of the search results. You'll get a lot of hits, but it won't be shared. And content that isn't shared isn't heard. People "bounce" from trite, poorly written content because it's already everywhere.

• •

Three Tips for Earning Attention

1. Be useful. Provide new information or present a unique way of explaining old information.
2. Be memorable. Follow the Four Cs to create an optimally memorable message.

3. **Be sharable. If it's not shared, your content might kind of suck.**

· ·

Regularly publishing useful, memorable, and sharable content that speaks in a consistent tone should be a part of every marketer's mission statement. This cannot be overstated because you can't build a following if you have nothing to follow. Building a following requires being heard by more than those dropping in on the conversation occasionally, which means posting regularly increases the chances you'll be seen and shared.

To keep your audience engaged on social media, you must work on gaining and earning attention, as well as maintaining it. An effective mix of messages tells your audience what you do, how you do it, and even *why* you do it. It's not enough to slap up a few videos (glorified commercials for your brand) or announce new products. The ratio of educational, entertaining, or useful content should be at least four to five times higher than that of pure brand grandstanding. You can influence the decision-making process with endearing, enlightening, and empowering messages, drawing customers into your embrace with a compelling and authentic story, and then leaving them alone to make the choice.

We live in an incredibly media savvy world. Today's consumers can smell a snake and know when snake oil is the product being sold. Those same consumers increasingly shy away from companies whose messages focus on "the sell" while they lean in to the brands that "tell."

This is the Conversation Age. This is speaking human. This is, ultimately, the handshake moment that turns lurkers, leads, prospects, and gawkers into customers.

Icebreaker

Take a moment to think about you, your brand, and your own views of your company. How do you view your current brand personality? What would you change? What is the online culture you'd like to create or foster?

As an exercise in brainstorming, put together a list of words that describe your current brand personality and the personality you'd like to be. How far away are you from each of those traits? Think about the type of content that would begin to shift the focus to your thought leadership instead of your competition's.

Once you have a sense of where you want to be, start formalizing a content style guide around that personality. Describe the personality (witty, formal, sarcastic, friendly, straightforward, lighthearted, etc.). What are the nuances in your language that you can adopt regularly that would be found across all your content?

CHAPTER 2

Tell a Story

When you meet someone for the first time and the conversation begins, do you brag about your big home or the cool car you drive, or do you talk about where you're from or what you do for a living? If the former, you're talking about your features; if the latter, you're framing a story about who you are.

All of us, every day, are living out our own life stories. And storytelling is baked into our DNA. We naturally want to pass information on to each other for many reasons, not the least of which is to make sense of things and the world we live in. To make it easier to understand, and to remember the important parts. So, it stands to reason, to have a good conversation, you must tell a good story.

When companies publish content, often their first instinct is to focus on the company, their products and services (the what), and why they're awesome because the first box in the content checklist is to just get the content out there. What happens next? (Crickets chirping.) They end up publishing useless content. They're participating in the conversation, but no one is listening. Why?

Read the following examples on the super boring and complex subject of statistics. Which strikes a chord with you?

> *In statistics, mean refers to one measure of the central tendency either of a probability distribution or of the random variable characterized by that distribution. The mean is equal to the sum over every possible value weighted by the probability of that value.*[1]

Or this one?

> The Price Is Right *is the perfect game show for math geeks. . . . Each pricing game leading up to the much-anticipated "Showcase Showdown" relies primarily on the fact that most contestants guess somewhere in the middle on the price of a pack of gum or a new car—what's called a "mean" in statistical terms.*[2]

Unless you're a professor of statistics, I'm going to guess the second one sounds better, correct? The first example qualifies as content. The second is conversation wrapped in story. You may never need to know what a statistical mean is, but now you're less likely to forget within the next few days if asked. And that's the point.

How do you hold someone's attention long enough to break down a topic, engender his or her trust, so he or she remembers you and is left feeling a little smarter than a few minutes ago? The answer lies in good storytelling.

Historically Speaking

Think about it. The most successful books and movies tell a story well and draw readers and viewers in with ease. Architecture and art weave a story amid lines and design relating details of times past. Religions are filled with storytelling intended to impart wisdom. News outlets seek to tell stories designed to evoke emotions and encourage action. Even today, oral stories told through the ages are familiar to nearly everyone.

The art of storytelling is as old as time and continues to serve us as an effective vehicle for sharing information as well as building trustworthy relationships. Storytellers have long been respected and well-liked, defining and binding humanity.

The Power of Story

Human memory is narrative driven. We literally live in a story that is unfolding every day, and each experience we store in our brain has a story attached to it. To that end, storied narratives drive people, not features and benefits, or products and services.

When businesses engage marketing firms, they often utilize instant gratification to capture the audience's attention rather than employing lasting contentment or happiness to reach their audience. Though the two may seem synonymous, they aren't. Using contentment and happiness are the most valuable in attracting and keeping audience attention because those are the things that shape human narratives. The narrative (story) is the root of everything we are as humans because our stories are shaped by our experiences along with what we read and think about. In "The Pleasure/Happiness Gap," Seth Godin, marketing guru, explains:

> *Marketers usually sell pleasure. That's a short-cut to easy, repeated revenue. Getting some-one hooked on the hit that comes from caffeine, tobacco, video or sugar is a business model. . . .*
>
> *On the other hand, happiness is some-thing that's difficult to purchase. It requires more patience, more planning, and more con-fidence . . . we're more likely to find it with a mature, mindful series of choices, most of which have to do with seeking out connection and generosity. . . .*
>
> *More than ever before, we control our brains by controlling what we put into them. Choosing the media, the interactions, the sto-ries, and the substances we ingest changes what we experience.*[3]

And this is where your storytelling can set your brand apart. Unless you're inventing a time machine, you're likely selling a product or service in a competitive market with basic, valued attributes that you share with everyone else in your space—low prices, great service, quality products—and only a few key differentiators. Your content could serve as one of those differentiators that truly set you apart. The secret sauce of effective content lies in your ability to tap into human emotion through the power of story.

For companies and brands, the handshake moment at the business level is the way in which the world experiences a brand for the first time. If you don't tell your own story, the world will tell it for you, and it might not be pretty. Take, for example, the aftermath of the financial crisis of 2008–2009. The companies left standing because they were "too big to fail" had a tough road in regaining public trust, particularly because, up until that point, there was no narrative to guide public perception. There was brand recognition, of course, but few banks and financial institutions could make the claim they were well-received because of their altruistic sensibilities. Nope, the public categorically decided for them—and the broad consensus was they were the bad guys.

● ●

Goldman Sachs Progress Campaign:
A Case Study

Goldman Sachs's Progress Campaign came about mainly because they never created their brand story and the market had begun to create it for them as well. The campaign "Progress Is Everyone's Business" began in an effort, not to win new clients for the firm, but instead to temper public perception to inform people how investments can be used by companies for the good of the nation and the world. The first advertisement featured a photo of wind turbines (representing renewable energy) and a close-up of a worker in a hard hat standing at the base of one of the turbines.

The ads that followed continued to tell the stories of the work Goldman Sachs has done for the good of the country and the globe, including large investments in bio research and relief efforts in areas of natural disaster. The goal of the ads is education and inspiration. Goldman Sachs stepped back, got out of its own way, and offered profiles of companies in which it had invested, and the positive changes made by those companies around the world. It was a far cry from their typical advertising, which featured dry talking heads discussing investment banking.

The stories featured in the campaign as of this writing include MuleSoft, Newark, New Orleans, and Western & Southern.[4] MuleSoft has worked to connect systems and allow for greater accessibility to information and continued progress in IT for companies large and small. In Newark, investments in education, housing, and jobs, are driving a renaissance in the city. In New Orleans, investments in the community and economy have aided in the city's recovery from natural disaster. Investments made in Western & Southern have permitted what began as a small hometown firm to help Americans plan for their future in innovative ways. Each of these stories, and many more like them, continue to help Goldman Sachs create a positive buzz while showing their human value to ordinary consumers and making a connection.

Your Story

Goldman Sachs discovered that creating a brand story helped the world understand they were in fact helping people all across the country as a direct result of investments. Your story should do the same, instantly and effectively communicating your history, your values, your beliefs, and more. And it's that story—your real story—that earns the attention and admiration of your audience. Your story shouldn't be filled with jargon and other gibberish but must be communicated in authentic language. Your truth and the genuineness of your story are the hook that gains the loyalty of your following. They are what shines through in your content. Your story should be so candid and straightforward that your audience completely forgets they are reading a business blog about your brand.

To accomplish this goal, you must remember that human beings literally live in story. Most businesses think they're data driven, but what truly drives a company (at the core) is its narrative. Without the narrative, the only thing a company has is the what, not the why. Eventually, a company that markets products and services alone without a narrative is susceptible to a negative disruption. Their brand has never clarified what they're doing and why they're doing it, and their audience has no idea who they are.

Think about it: Apple's story isn't about selling great computers; it's about innovation. Volvo's story isn't about luxury cars; it's a narrative entrenched in keeping families safe and together. Uber isn't selling fast rides; they're changing the way the world travels. You'd be hard pressed to find an ad or a single word of content that only discusses the features and benefits of their products from any of these firms.

Why Storytelling?

Storytelling, at its heart, is an essential human activity that must be the cornerstone of any meaningful content strategy. It's the ideal channel to capture audience attention and keep it. As Eileen Sutton, one of today's great brand story architects, so eloquently put it, "If the story is the nest, the content becomes the baby starlings hatching, growing strong, and flying off as they carry compelling messages to everyone. Stories are fundamental to culture, to society, and to every individual life."[5] There are several benefits of story to consider:

1. A story translates complex data through a narrative lens. Instead of talking about the topic, product, or service, wrap a story around the data and make it more human. Bring it down to eye level for the audience. Appeal to their mind and heart through feelings and emotions, not facts and data. Your story makes the subject understandable, relatable, and more memorable to the audience. Not only will they understand your story, they're more likely to do something meaningful with it. (This is the holy grail of conversation marketing.)

2. No one can argue with a story. As soon as we hear facts and data, our brain immediately begins to argue with them. In contrast, your personal experience or someone else's story is true—and persuasive. It may not move us, and it may even make us angry. But we can't argue with it. A story is processed in a completely different way than data-driven facts.

3. A story elicits an emotional response. And that's a good thing. Emotions easily influence people. You may not remember what someone said to you today a year from

now, but you'll remember how they made you feel. You will remember the emotion you felt when you interacted with them, and that can be a powerful igniter of action.

4. With a story, the brain turns cacophony into song. There's a rhythm to external messages that repeat over time, and the human brain normalizes them. If those messages are bad and we hear them repeated, they become normalized and ignored. The best example of this are negative political campaign ads that have driven our elections at every level for decades. On the other hand, a storied narrative that touches the hearts of the audience, becomes a harmony that is embedded in our minds. We are reminded of it in a positive way every time we hear it and listen as if we are hearing it for the first time.

Market From the Inside Out

This honest narrative you're trying to tell means marketing from the inside out. You aren't simply spewing words, but rather sharing the true story of your brand. You are sharing your rich history and what sets you apart in both philosophy and purpose. To do it, you must dig deep. True storied marketing must convey your brand values as well as your corporate ethics, explaining why your brand is the unsung hero of your industry.

● ●

Chipotle: A Case Study

Chipotle's "The Scarecrow" video was not a feel-good fairytale story, but rather an effort on behalf of the brand to effectively tell the true story of Chipotle's beliefs in the ethical treatment of animals. The story, as it was told in a YouTube video, evoked powerful emotions, even angering viewers to make the point that Chipotle is a brand built on foundation of good nutrition, animal rights, and corporate ethics.[6]

And though it never aired on television, the video received more than 13.5 million views on YouTube, and its companion game app became an overnight success. It garnered overwhelming media attention, raised intense ire in the food processing industry, and effectively told the mission of the Chipotle brand, serving "food with integrity."

Chipotle in "The Scarecrow" brought their message to the people via social media and successfully connected their message to their brand, engaging emotions along the way. Chipotle told a story, in old-fashioned narrative form, that provoked emotion from those who agreed with them and those who vehemently opposed their message. And the outcome was that those who railed against the story actually created a stronger bond of those in agreement to the Chipotle brand. "The Scarecrow" narrative simply began the conversation and carried the story to the people.

In addition, Chipotle spent no money on advertising "The Scarecrow" but rather counted on social media shares to carry their message to their audience by the most effective means possible. In this case, Chipotle's cause and the essence of the brand meshed perfectly, effectively supporting their mission, "food with integrity," while allowing the story to grow and spread to millions.

• •

The Story Starts the Conversation

Chipotle used "The Scarecrow" as a storied tale that aligned the message of their cause perfectly with their brand and in doing so started a conversation among millions. "The Scarecrow" became an effective marketing tool for their message and their brand as it engaged audiences on both sides of the conversation.

The task was accomplished, first and foremost, by keeping their target audience in mind throughout the story. Any marketing campaign is only as successful as the power it has to generate a healthy and relatable conversation with the target audience based on the story being told.

When creating your story relaying your message to the audience, use content channels specific to your business. Chipotle had successfully used YouTube in the past and understood its power to reach the audience in a grassroots effort that would be driven by effectively by that audience. The word was then spread about Chipotle's cause (animal rights) and message ("food with integrity"), reaching new customers on the recommendation (shares) of current followers. Your story may be ideally suited for YouTube distribution or may be more effective using other content channels (Facebook, Instagram, Twitter, a blog, a newsletter, a microsite). Once your story is told in a relevant way, you have created a base from which you can launch on other content/communication/social channels.

As you continue to tell your story, you must monitor audience engagement. Analyze your target audience's responses as well as the actions they take as a result of your story. You can use a number of analytical tools to accomplish this task: following audience purchasing and its origin; gaining an understanding of what drives your audience, what turns them off, and what piques their interest and instigates a positive exchange or transaction. Remember: Your goal is not necessarily the number of clicks to purchase, but a connection and a call to action by your audience. It is the customer's journey that brings them to align with your story, your mission, and your brand that you're seeking.

As you share your story, you must remember there is never a "one size fits all" scenario. Your potential customers—your target audiences—are looking for sincerity, energy, honesty—a story they can relate to and one that seems to be told specifically for them, not to the masses. In order to achieve that kind of storytelling success, you must know your audience, of whom no two are alike. And this requires research and well-thought-out storytelling that has the ability to connect with your customers, engage them, and motivate action beyond hearing your story.

You have a global audience, but you must keep in mind your story is only heard by one person at a time and your goal is to gain a customer for life, not simply a single sale. To achieve that goal, you must learn to infuse storytelling into your content.

How to Infuse Storytelling into Your Content

We've talked a lot about storytelling from a brand story perspective. No doubt you've heard a great deal of chatter among your peers about the need to infuse storytelling into your content marketing. After all, with so many companies-turned-publishers, it stands to reason that if you're putting out content, you should be a good storyteller. But the sad truth is, many are not.

As important as storytelling is for your content, it's largely misunderstood in practice. Gaining the knowledge and understanding of storytelling will give you an edge. Among the daily noise, a good story with an immediate impact is key.

The problem with talking about storytelling is that you might assume you have to craft a novel every time you publish an article. This just isn't true. What matters is using simple storytelling techniques to develop your article so your content resonates with readers and elicits an emotional response of some kind. This doesn't have to happen with only a single article. After all, you're adding to or starting a conversation, which takes place over time, through many pieces of content, possibly across multiple channels.

Not every article has to follow a story format. It's the rules of storytelling that matter the most, not the structure of the story itself. The key is, in every piece, long or short, to borrow from storytelling techniques to develop the stories and content that becomes your brand story.

. . . .

Storytelling Techniques for Content

1. Don't talk about yourself. You are not the hero of the story. Your customer is.
2. Incite an emotional response. Anger, sadness, laughter, joy—it doesn't matter. Our emotions create memories that linger. People may argue with the ideas, but they won't forget.
3. Use metaphors and analogies. They help your audience to relate to the subject in a human way.
4. Inspire. Give purpose to what you do. If you're writing about a product or service or activity, readers should feel it will have a positive impact in their lives. This isn't done with press releases. It's done with story.
5. Avoid jargon. Jack didn't climb a deciduous vine found in the legume family. He climbed a beanstalk.
6. Don't "over-story." Remember you're dealing with short attention spans, particularly online. It's not a tome; it's content using storytelling techniques.

7. Create something shareable. If you can tap into an emotional response, you've created content that will be shared. Viral is your best friend in content.

• •

Consider Proctor and Gamble's "Share the Load" campaign, which utilized these storytelling techniques to create a message that was eventually heard around the globe.

• •

Share the Load: A Case Study

The #SharetheLoad campaign of Ariel India, P&G, BBDO Worldwide inspired millions across the globe by breaking down gender stereotypes, showing how male household members' actions can create greater equality in the home. The video story begins with a father watching his grown-up daughter rush in from work and begin making dinner, doing laundry, and taking care of the members of her household while her husband watches television. The father quickly realizes his daughter's family is following the example he set when she was growing up, along with the example her father-in-law demonstrated to her husband.

As realization sweeps over him, he apologizes for not telling her that taking care of the house was not her job alone. He heads home to his wife, leaving a note of apology for his daughter. As he arrives home, he gathers his clothes from his suitcase and heads to the washing machine, much to the surprise of his wife. The story ends with the line "Why is laundry only a mother's job?" superimposed over the Ariel Laundry Box.

The campaign, promoted by Sheryl Sandberg and Bill and Melinda Gates, garnered 12 million views and more than 300,000 shares, and proved a laundry detergent company can tell a simple human story and reach its audience effectively.[7] P&G's Ariel brand found a fresh approach to make their content more impactful by simply telling a story that resonated with around the world. Promoting gender equality and challenging gender stereotypes, the #SharetheLoad video worked to encourage men to share in the household chores. The campaign gained enormous attention which resulted in increased followers after Sheryl Sandberg, Facebook COO, activist, and author, shared the video on her Facebook page. The post quickly rose to among the top three most-shared brand posts in a single month. Following Sandberg's lead, Bill and Melinda Gates as well as Robert Scoble shared the post.

The message of #SharetheLoad quickly spread across other social media channels, further expanding the story's audience and keeping the conversation going and growing. Quite simply, #SharetheLoad is a prime example of delivering brand philosophy in story form in a creative and engaging manner. P&G is a conglomerate sharing a purpose and succeeding.

• •

Final Thoughts

You may be asking, "If storytelling is so great, why isn't every company doing it?" The main reason is because it challenges the marketing status quo and most people are uncomfortable going outside their comfort zone. Crafting your unique brand story negates established storylines even if those stories are fragmented and weak (we're the biggest, we're the oldest, etc.).

Creating a likeable personality and developing a tone that engenders trust involve good storytelling techniques that are authentic. When you do, you can effectively reach your audience with creative storytelling that shares your mission and goals, while promoting your brand.

Icebreaker

Think about a pain point your company addresses (your solution to your industry's problem). What is a situation your audience might find themselves in that you can craft a simple story around?

Answer these questions to sketch out a story framework:

1. Who are the hero and villain? (Hint: It's not you, your brand, or your products/services.)
2. What is the setup?
3. What is the conflict?
4. What is the unexpected twist? (What can you tell them that hasn't already been said?)
5. What is the resolution (the save, what they need to know)?
6. Finally, what is the punchline? (This is the call to action. What do you want them to do next? Hint: Don't ask them to buy anything, yet.)

As you write your story, try not to mention your company or your product. Get to the heart of the problem and create your best prose!

CHAPTER 3

Stay Humble

As counterintuitive as it may seem, it's time to slow back down to a time when all selling, much like politics, was conducted on a local level. Customers weren't "audiences" or "targets" then; they were neighbors, friends, community members, and family. The waitress at the diner remembered your regular morning breakfast order. The butcher knew who preferred which cut of meat before they ever set foot in their store. These people were part of their customers' everyday lives in reactive, mirroring ways that today's brands seem to fall short of.

In the absence of this old-school face-to-face interaction, how do you translate that same personal touch as your local butcher?

1. Be approachable.
2. Focus on your audience's pain points.

3.   Know a thing or two about steak.
4.   Don't talk about yourself.

Because humility was a large part of that relationship, the focus was outward-facing on the customer, not inward-focused on sales. Being humble means you kill the id. There is no me, me, me. All the focus is on the customer and their needs, and their understanding of the difference you make in their lives.

Humility is defined as being free from pride and arrogance. It is a quality that is often lacking in present-day advertising that beats consumers over the head with the fabulous features and benefits of your products and services. The consumers don't truly care about your pride in your products and services, but more importantly care about how you and your brand improve their lives. They want to know *why* you do what you do.

Ditch the Id

Being humble begins, as mentioned, with letting go of your ego—that instinctual part of your psyche that screams for you as a marketer to make noise for your products or services. Resist the urge. The id wants to tell the world how great you and your products are, and how great they are for buying them. To be a good storyteller, you have to kill the id.

Killing the id is easy. Simply stop talking about you. Stop selling. It doesn't matter that you might have the fastest-growing company in the industry or that you're the "leader in your space." Nobody's listening. Instead, harness a different approach—the one that shows your human value as well as your customers'. Provide insight on what you've done to impact your customers' lives rather than what they've done for you. Social media was created around the idea of sharing human currency, not for using it as a bully pulpit for selling.

To accomplish this, you tell stories (Chapter 2)—stories about life, not about you or your origin story, that resonate with your audience's experiences. You then curate those experiences into useful, colorful, and creative applications that engage your customers. With the stories, you build trust, rather than pitch products. When you simply pitch your products at every turn, you become white noise, which begs the consumer to stop listening and tune you out.

If, instead, you ask, "How can I help you?" in every story you tell, the hero of the story shifts from being your products or services and becomes your customers. And your customers' point of view is the only one that matters!

Tell your story to your customers and potential customers—the story of what you and your products have done to improve their lives, the lives of those who have helped you become the success you're today.

Pop quiz:

1. Who are you likely going to enjoy talking to more at a party of strangers? The person droning on about his achievements? Or the

one who engages you in a story about his friends?

2. Do you think you learn something from both? Yes, but what is the more productive lesson? Which one are you likely to trust more? Which are you more likely to stick around for just a little longer?

The absence of self is a powerful marketing tool. The things not said about you and your brand in your content and advertising speak volumes about the degree to which your audience can trust you and your brand. Trust builds relationships. Relationships build partnerships. And this leads to another truth.

Don't Pitch. Teach.

Now, apart from noting exactly what you're offering them, customers today also understand what you're *not* offering them. Audiences today are quite perceptive and notice aspects of your messaging, such as your tone. (Is it prideful or humble?) They also can tell if you're bullying them to buy your product or inviting them in for a friendly conversation filled with relevant information. The point here: Don't pitch. Teach. Be humble, and create human value that inspires your audience to action.

It all starts with teachable stories that show your human value the world. To begin telling your story, consider this: How do your company and your products/services make a difference in the lives of the people you service? Now ask yourself, "What can I teach that solves problems?" As Joe Pulizzi stated in the foreword of this book, you want to "deliver valuable content without asking your audience to buy anything." Think of your content as an extension of your product line. Nobody really cares about your products and services. They care about how you make a difference in their lives. People want to know why you do what you do, not all the features of your products and services. You teach them by shifting the focus to your customers and prospects, and away from you and your products.

If you've launched your amazing content marketing strategy and it's falling short of your expectations, the shortfall may be a result of your delivery. If your prospects are responding with silence to your efforts, ask yourself, "Did we pitch rather than teach?"

Consumers around the globe are looking for heart, for help, for humanity, for an ideology they can get behind. Are you showing them the "human" value of your brand? Or maybe you just reconstituted your content with the proclamation of "customers come here first"? Your content probably tells your audience exactly what you do or what you sell, but does it tell then who *you* are?

Think about it. You, like everyone else, make snap judgments every day. You look to visual clues, voice tones, facial expressions, speech patterns, the clothing and the body language of those you meet to decide if you can trust them, relate to them, or have a connection with them. Your audience is doing the same thing with the brands they come in contact with on a daily basis. Knowing that, take a look at your content from the thirty-thousand-foot view. Are you sharing the importance of your brand's human value? Are you making an attempt to improve the lives of your customers even a little bit? Further, what are the handshake moments your brand is making, regardless of the channel in which it's delivered? Each is just like a face-to-face encounter, and you need to know that you're projecting your human value in every encounter, no matter how brief.

If you're teaching and not pitching, you give your audience something to talk about and start the conversation. You need to tell a true story that speaks to your human value while you engage customers "eye to eye," revealing the identity and the humanity of your brand.

Telling the *Right* Story

Most of the time, telling the right story (Chapter 2) is eclipsed by giving the wrong messaging. Consider this scenario. You sell insurance. You publish a blog post about the difference between term and whole life insurance. Then you go on to write that if they "click" now, they can get a free, in-home consultation.

Really? Your customer can get that same information from a quick online search. So, how does the information in an article that merely defines two types of insurance inspire action? Although the topic may be important, it's unoriginal, and asking for the sale without a concerted effort to connect emotionally with the audience is not honoring the readers' time with you.

Most people understand why they need home and car insurance. But facing mortality, let alone the value of your life can be difficult, particularly for someone in their twenties. A better approach might be to discuss some of the benefits of life insurance for the living! Farmers Insurance created Farmers Inner Circle to address such topics. One article from the blog did so without ever asking for a sale. In fact, you won't even find a call to action in some of the articles, such as "How Life Insurance Can Help Provide Stability for Millennials." The branding here is passive and inferred. Farmers wouldn't write an article about a product it can't sell that would put it at a competitive disadvantage. It exercises humility and educates its audience with a twist on how to use life insurance now, not later for its intended purpose. Now, I'm intrigued.

The point is, you have to write to your audience, not simply fill a page, and address your customers' needs. You're addressing their pain points and serving them by solving a problem, sometimes problems they don't know they have. In this scenario, your potential customer just needs information right now. The sale will come later. When prospects are viewing and reading your content, captivate them with it. Give them the opportunity to take action on their terms, even if it's only getting more information. If you're having a problem remembering what their terms are, it's simple:

1. Don't talk about you. Talk about me.
2. Don't sell me anything.
3. Do educate, entertain, or delight me with something meaningful.

To Be Humble Is to Be Human

Let's take a few minutes to explore the human value in you, your brand, and your business. Begin with this question: *How does your company make a positive difference in the world through its products and services?* As you consider your response, remember it's not about how great your products or services are. It is not about how you're better than the competition.

What is it about, then? It is about your humility and your human value—all the ways you, your company, and your brand contribute to making the world a better place whether at the local, national, or international level.

Let these critical strategies guide you as you tell your story, engaging your audience with education, information, and inspiration.

- Highlight your vulnerability to your customers and win their appreciation for your honesty. Speak human and be humble, and they'll return the favor tenfold.
- You don't need to shout your story with megaphones, slogans, or noise. No matter how big you are, there are people meeting

you for the first time. Be mindful of what you say and how you say it, always displaying your humility, openness, and truth. Everything else is simply noise, to be tuned out.

- Customers don't grade on a positive curve because you're bigger than the competition. They expect humility and don't respond well to "corporate-speak."

- Speak to your audience as if you were one of them; always focus on them, not you. This makes you approachable to your customers so it's easier for them to reach out to you when they need your help.

- Provide cures for their pain points, even if they don't involve your product. All good content strategies ultimately lead to trusting you as you focus on their needs, not yours.

Icebreaker

Great conversations are about sharing, not bragging. Think about the last cocktail party you attended. Remember that one guy who couldn't stop talking about himself? Sure, there was lots of talking, but he never really said anything of value. Well, this could be you, if every third sentence you speak or write is about how great you, your company, or your company's products are.

You can easily tell if you're humbly teaching or pitching arrogantly by taking an inventory of your existing content and performing a self-assessment ("self" meaning your company). Take any article, white paper, or video script you classify as "content" for public consumption and count how many times your product or company name is mentioned. One or two is ideal, but in all likelihood, you have more. When you get to three or four mentions, your customer is likely shutting you and your message down.

Try to rewrite it as a short, educational blog post without mentioning a thing about your company, product, or service. Don't sell. Just teach.

CHAPTER 4

Pick Your Party

So far, the discussion has centered on how to join in and have a meaningful conversation with your audience. Here, the discussion moves from the rules of engagement in your conversation to the venue (i.e., choosing your channels). Equally important to the *how* of your conversation is the *where*. It should all fit seamlessly together when you think about it; part of learning how to talk to your audience and engage them in conversation is deciding where to talk to them in the first place. In essence, you have to pick your party.

Your content marketing strategy consists of multiple touch points along the path to purchase, all part of a content ecosystem. The conversation you are having as part of your content marketing strategy doesn't begin and end with your individual channels. Even though it's possible to get a sale or track business from a single channel, that isn't the primary goal of the channel, nor should it be. Each of your channels serves a unique purpose, with one channel leading into another. That said, whether you utilize one channel or multiple channels working together, content marketing takes time. As you know well, no path to purchase is a straight line.

• •

What's Everyone Else Doing?

These are the top five channels B2C marketers use to distribute content:

1. Social media: 89 percent.
2. Email: 86 percent.
3. Blogs: 70 percent.
4. In-person events: 42 percent.
5. Print (other than magazines): 34 percent.

These are the top content types B2C marketers are using in those content marketing channels:

1. Social media posts: 96 percent.
2. Videos (pre-produced): 76 percent.
3. Illustrations/photos: 67 percent.
4. Infographics: 59 percent.
5. Interactive tools (quizzes, assessments, calculators): 38 percent.[1]

• •

Forget About the Sale (for the Moment)

You're earning a relationship with your audience, not buying one. In content marketing, the path to purchase is not a straight line. As mentioned at the beginning of the chapter, your content marketing strategy does not begin and end with a single channel. Remember that your content is created to attract and retain your customers. It's not your point of sale. Instead, your content channel is your sales incubator.

That's not to say you won't win a few sales in one take with a single piece of content. I'm simply arguing that a few sales successes from a single piece of content would be the exception, not the rule. A billboard on a highway only drives sales if someone is hungry and sees a McDonald's ad for fifty-cent Big Macs. That's great for quick pops. But a well-thought-out channel strategy in content marketing is intended to nurture a relationship, bring a captive audience closer to your brand, and evoke meaningful action or engagement from that audience.

First, you must set a realistic goal for your content.

Weak: "Let's start a blog to generate sales."

Better: "Let's engage our clients with a blog, build an audience, earn their trust, and provide them value in the short term, as well as the long term."

By way of example, absent the sale, some key performance indicators (KPIs) of a blog that would determine success right out of the gate are:

1. Traffic: How many people come to the site, from where (other sites, inbound links, influencers), and how (devices like mobile, tablet, etc.)?
2. Engagement: Did they leave right away (bounce rate)? How long did they stay? How many pages did they read? Where did they go from there?
3. Effectiveness: What did they do when they got there? Did they respond to your call to action? Did they share it?

Pitching products is widely accepted in more traditional "bullhorn" marketing channels such as TV, radio, newspapers, and magazines. And it's appropriate on your own website—just not your blog. Though any channel can be used for both bullhorn and conversation marketing, the following is a cheat sheet to remind you which channels are better suited for tooting your own horn versus having a conversation.

Bullhorn Marketing	Conversation Marketing
TV	Blogs
Radio	Videos
Newspaper	Social media
Magazines	Microsites
Company website (not a blog)	Podcasts
Email	Native advertising

Bullhorn Marketing	Conversation Marketing
Billboards	Digital newsletters
	White papers
	Print magazines
	Digital magazines
	Books
	Ebooks
	Webinars

How to Create Your Channel Plan

When you begin to create your channel distribution plan, you start by asking: "What am I trying to accomplish?" Dig deeper than simply "We want to generate sales from our content." Instead, focus your attention on a solid engagement goal like "We want to be the top-ranked site to address pain points for welding suppliers."

Next, ask yourself: "How do we want to get there?" All the while keep in mind it's not a straight line. What is your content marketing strategy designed to accomplish?

Then, determine where your customers are hanging out. Use all the research tools at your disposal, including surveys, direct calls (calling your customers personally to ask), keywords, social media listening, trolling social media, and industry blogs.

The final step in your channel strategy is the development of the channels themselves. In the beginning, cast a wide net, but choose your channels wisely. Not everyone needs a Facebook, Twitter, and LinkedIn channel, for example. The need for all of them is overblown, so you'll want to answer two important questions:

1. Why do you need this channel? and
2. How does this channel fit into our goal?

For example, if you're a B2B business, LinkedIn, a place where other professionals in your industry are seeking out information and expertise, might be a good channel to focus your resources. On the other hand, if you're a B2C business, Facebook or Instagram might be a place to focus your resources to reach your audience.

In Detail: A Content Marketing Channel Plan

As you develop your channel distribution plan, there are multiple factors to consider. You should start with an examination of your current position to decide where your story will have the most impact on your audience. Note the content marketing strategies you already have in place (website, blog, Facebook, etc.) relative to where (Instagram, LinkedIn, a new blog, etc.) you'd like to see your latest efforts succeed. Once you have a handle on your current situation, consider what you need to change, stop, or add to more effectively tell your story. From these factors, you can set new priorities and goals.

Next, consider each channel's objectives in relation to one another. Where do your objectives need an overhaul? What channels overlap with one another, and is there a way to make that overlap more effective? Now determine how to make your channel objectives effectively accomplish your goals.

Now, for each channel you've identified, you need to plan your content to tell your story in a way that reaches the audience specific to that channel. The content may be different to reach the audience at each channel, but your story should be consistent throughout all channels. With each channel, you will need to identify audience members in order to reach them effectively, keeping in mind that on social media you may want more than one account to reach each unique following. Whether you are building community on Facebook or delivering sought-out information on LinkedIn, your content and your context should focus on each unique audience while maintaining the integrity of your story within the conversation.

For each channel, as well as the overlapping channels, you need to identify and understand the goals for each channel (e.g., 100 new Facebook followers in a month, fifty shares of an informative article on LinkedIn, etc.). Once you identify the goals, ensure that you have the people as well as the tools to manage the content and conversation on each channel.

Finally, your channel distribution plan needs a schedule or a calendar to define the factors needs to achieve your goals. Each channel's schedule should include a posting schedule for content, a unique tone and structure, as well as the action you hope to gain from the audience.

As an example, here's a hypothetical content marketing channel strategy you might take if you're a B2B firm:

1. Create a social media presence on LinkedIn.
2. Start blogging on the influencer pages to build an audience.
3. Begin sending your audience to deep links on your company's own blog (your primary content source).
4. Add calls to action (CTAs), embedded links, and lead generation devices (e.g., newsletter sign-ups) in your blog posts asking your readers to do something. (Prospects could remain here for some time.)
5. Ask for the sale on your site.

The process from Step 1 to Step 5 could all take one day or many months. It all depends on how you execute your strategy, how well you're telling your story overall, and how well-crafted your content is.

Remember that every company is different, and your channel distribution plan won't look exactly like anyone else's. To achieve your goals, you will likely need to experiment, seek feedback, and continue to make changes along the way.

A Tentacled "Conversation Ecosystem"

Your channel strategy should be a tentacled "conversation ecosystem" of multiple conversations. As previously mentioned, you have to cast a wide net of channels that play off one another. One channel starts a conversation and then leads to another channel, though they remain interconnected. Media companies and toy manufacturers have this down to a science, including LEGO and the action/superhero franchises like Marvel/DC.

●●●

LEGO: A Case Study

One of the most powerful and successful channel strategies in content marketing has been LEGO. Hands down. Their channel plan spans social media, websites, microsites, print magazines, cinema, television shows, and YouTube, ultimately developing a content juggernaut of story worlds, "must have" characters, and more.

In the 1980s and the decade that followed, after LEGO's patent expired in 1983, LEGO faced a massive threat from toy companies, large and small, seeking to sell virtual duplicates of their construction blocks.[2] LEGO fought back with an integrated marketing plan that enveloped multiple channels successfully. Today, LEGO is among the most successful toy companies in the world running their content marketing plan in the style of a powerhouse media giant utilizing these channels effectively. Here is a sampling of the channels in LEGO's content marketing strategy:

1. Every LEGO story, from *Star Wars* to Marvel superheros, offers the audience a microsite dedicated not only to retailing, but with featured

movies, polls, games, and quizzes that share plot and character secrets.

2. As new storylines go live, LEGO presents a miniseries movie on cable, which follows later on the LEGO website.

3. *LEGO Club Magazine,* the latest rendering of the original *Brick Kick* magazine first released in 1987. Popular among LEGO fans, this magazine is tailored for readers by age and market.

4. LEGOLAND Theme Parks were developed in partnership with Merlin Entertainments Group. Currently there are eight parks and discovery centers galore.

5. LEGO invites fans and friends to Click, the LEGO community platform, where they can share their LEGO creations, play games, download apps, and enjoy LEGO stories.

6. The LEGO social network is designed just for kids and is loaded with parental controls and LEGO safety measures (which include background checks for moderators). Kids on the network can create their own unique pages, meet other LEGO kids, watch LEGO TV, and win rewards. LEGO doesn't engage kids on traditional social media but invites kids under thirteen here to share and enjoy the unique LEGO community.[3]

7. LEGO holds "Club" meetings in its stores for members around the globe who enjoy theme activities and building with other LEGO fans.

8. LEGO users can sign up for the free LEGO ID and gain access to multiplayer games, create a personal page, and share their creations on LEGO galleries.

LEGO, of course, has a premium-quality product line loved by adults and children around the world, but LEGO's conversation, communication, and content with those fans tells the story. LEGO generates and distributes content that supports the company's goal of selling more products by attracting and retaining customers (like a toy company) as well as generating direct revenue (like a media company) though movies, cartoons, licensing fees, books, and games. The ultimate channel strategy at LEGO is to connect and build relationships with their audience members—children, teens, parents, fans, shoppers, and consumers—using various methods based on what they enjoy (building LEGOs) and the fact that the audience wants to share their LEGO creations with others.[4] The result is a variety of channels with tailored content that sometimes overlaps (as seen above), but is always targeted based on search results, both paid and organic. Ultimately, whereever their audience is engaged, LEGO works to protect the brand in the conversation while continuing to tell their story in ways that are both simple and complex, but always unified.

Embrace Channels for What They Are Today

As you pick your party and develop your channel distribution strategy, you have to embrace the channels for what they've become today, not what they once were. Think about it: Instagram isn't just for photos anymore, and the YouTube of today is not the video-sharing website it was when it started. It has become a massive, unregulated global television network.

Samsung Malaysia embraced YouTube with a miniseries of videos of their own. The series follows a tribute band about to get their "big break" when their lead singer, who not only has to leave the country, falls ill two weeks prior to their showcase performance. Samsung understood that you have to think about YouTube as a media platform beyond cat videos and novelty. It can be an effective channel strategy for those who jump into a high-quality, storytelling visual content realm. Not one person discusses Samsung the brand, but the video clearly demonstrates how the brand's products (mostly their smartphones) could be used in smart ways to help you in your life (or in this case, save the band).

Putting It All Together: The Editorial Calendar

The time has come to pull all this information together, and to do it, you need to organize and create an *editorial calendar* for your channel distribution strategy. If you've never used one, an editorial calendar is a tool that helps you manage a single conversation or multiple ones across one or more channels, for at least the next month or two (likely more). The editorial calendar should also guide your team on strategy, topic, frequency, and schedule of the content you intend to create.

Whether you prefer an uncomplicated spreadsheet or a detailed interactive calendar for your content production and distribution, your editorial calendar will be unique to your brand. To begin your editorial calendar creation, start by gathering information from your content marketing plan. Your audience is priority one, so stay focused on their information needs while you determine your content goals (leads, attendance, etc.). As you plan what, where, and how often to publish, keep in mind your team and their expertise as well as your resources and what limitations you have. Will you be using in-house staff or outsourcing your content?

Armed with that information, you can begin setting up your editorial calendar. You may want to start simply with an Excel spreadsheet or a Google Sheet, but if you choose to go with a calendar app, you'll find many that offer not only calendar tools, but collaboration tools as well (e.g., Trello, CoSchedule, Google Calendar, etc.). Most important is that the editorial calendar can be easily designed, shared, and accessed by your team. Your editorial calendar will have unique fields, but everyone can benefit from some uniform fields like these: date of content publication, content title/topic, content author, business stakeholder, status of content. In addition, you may want to add fields to track details like content formats, keywords (SEO), visuals (images, logos, etc.), platforms (channels), URLs, velocity (time tables), calls to action, impact, and even goals.

Your editorial calendar is now ready to go, and it's up to you to keep it filled with content topics and ideas that keep the conversation going with your audience. A calendar filled with ideas will help you manage and streamline content, and manage your workflow and publication schedule across all your channels, all the while keeping you and your brand moving in the right direction.

Icebreaker

As you prepare your next campaign, answer these questions to engage your audience, start a conversation, and bring about positive actions as a result.

1. Where are your customers "hanging out" online? You either know this or need to research this using data sources (such as the listening tools that we will cover in Chapter 6).
2. What are the most effective content channels for your niche? Where can you best reach potential customers who may be unaware of your message and your brand? It may be YouTube, Facebook, Twitter, Instagram, a traditional blog, a newsletter, or even a microsite.

PART TWO
TALKING

What we say and how we say it can make the difference between virality and silence. What are you going to talk about that hasn't already been said? When your audience shares something you said with someone else, you've gotten through to them. They now trust you just a little more than they did before they heard you. How will you keep the conversation going?

CHAPTER 5

Be Relevant (on a Molecular Level)

In the same way that each individual's DNA is unique, so is each member of your audience, and subsequently each and every one of your customers. As the discussion for being relevant begins, you will learn from basic examples the techniques you need to think of each person as an entire audience—in and of themselves.

In the previous chapter, you learned the importance of stepping back and listening intently to your audience. Here, you will learn how to put that advice into action. Listening is all about looking before you leap, and being relevant is making sure you're talking about the topics that interest your audience by addressing their pain points. Being relevant means speaking to their pain points in a language they understand. It's about remembering that no matter the size of the audience you're talking to, there is only one person at a time on the other side of the screen hearing your message.

Because you've listened, you'll find you have different segments (e.g., men versus women, traders versus investors, general practitioners versus medical specialists, and so on). And every bit of content you produce must be personalized to provide choices for those people, whether you're sending out magazines or emailing the link to your blog. You could deliver choices via a switch at the top of the home of your blog that says "men/women" or "investor/trader."

You can use tricks to personalize the language of your articles, making each reader feel as if you're speaking directly to them. Remember: The uniqueness of DNA is the perfect analogy for each of your customers. And by keeping that point in mind, you can treat each individual as they are—a unique member of your audience. It begins with the validation of their pain, not your gain. You have to talk less about yourself and more about the individuals in your audience. Next, you have to stop yourself from trying to cast a wide net, and instead discuss in detail the points that are relevant to your audience. Then, you have to remember to speak their language; after all "you're trying to create a meaningful dialogue between yourself and your audience members, a credible, genuine conversation that resonates with them."[1] Don't make you language too complicated or invent words. Use words your audience understands. Finally, you have to be a storyteller, because stories are relevant.

● ●

Old Spice: A Case Study

One of the first branded molecular campaigns in social media that enjoyed enormous success was created by Old Spice. In 2010, responding to increased competition in the marketplace, and an attempt to eschew irrelevancy, Old Spice launched an advertising campaign known as "Smell Like a Man, Man." The original ad, featuring actor and former NFL wide receiver Isaiah Mustafa, used its simple phrasing to reach both men and women and start a conversation. Except this conversation started as a slick, funny commercial. Launched just before the Super Bowl, the ad quickly went viral, enhancing Old Spice sales, and single-handedly revived the brand.

In June 2010, Old Spice continued the conversation with "Smell Like a Man, Man—the Sequel." This campaign invited consumers to ask questions via Facebook and Twitter, which the Old Spice Guy would answer personally. During the forty-eight-hour question window, more than 2,000 people responded with questions. Old Spice Guy then personally responded with two hundred answers via video on YouTube.[2] The responses, which set records for consumer engagement, went out to fans and celebrities like Kevin Rose, Alyssa Milano, Ashton Kutcher, and George Stephanopoulos.

On the first day, the response video garnered 5.9 million YouTube views (more than President Obama's victory speech); within the week that number was more than 40 million views, and within the month, Old Spice sales had risen 125 percent.[3] And on top of that, the conversation Old Spice Guy began continues with more than 105 million YouTube views of the campaign, a 300 percent increase in Old Spice website traffic, an 800 percent increase in Facebook engagement, a 2,700 percent increase in Twitter followers, and 1.2 billion earned media impressions. Old Spice continues to hold its position as the number-one YouTube brand channel.[4]

Old Spice successfully spoke to its audience in a real, relevant way, with easy-to-understand language, and on a molecular level and reached millions in a conversation that continues today.

Imagine "Molecular" Customer Service

Imagine a place where you're not being served. Wouldn't it be great if you were in line and tweeting your discouragement in real time? "I'm in line at WeSave Bank and it sucks!"

What if WeSave Bank tweeted you right back to apologize and let you know which hours of the day might have the fewest number of people in line? This type of "molecular" customer service is a brand taking care of their customers at the individual level. One person at a time.

Because it is personalized, it immediately resonates with the person and moves them closer to enlightenment and trust in your brand. As they absorb more and more relevant content of yours, they become advocates of your brand and brand ambassadors. Even if they don't purchase something from you or hire your services, they will likely be sharing your content with someone who will.

Content marketing at the molecular level is making sure the right information (relevant content) is getting to each individual at the right time in the places they're hanging out. Conversation isn't just about writing stories in your content marketing strategy. It's taking care of each individual's information needs as quickly as possible. It could be on a live, public forum like Twitter, a personalized email campaign that sends you curated content that is most relevant to your tastes and purchase history, or just using smart SEO best practices so that your content is more easily found by those who need it most.

You may recall in Chapter 2 that a brand's "handshake moment" is what they choose to do when they reach out to their audience, perhaps for the first time. When we break down what is really happening here, it's not that the brand is talking to an audience, but the brand recognizes they're talking to people, one at a time, and in most cases, on the other side of a screen. Oreo understood this truth and pulled off a conversation with all the individuals who were watching the 2013 Super Bowl. And they did it with a simple tweet.

Oreo: A Case Study

On February 3, 2013, the power went out at the Superdome during Super Bowl play between the Francisco 49ers and the Baltimore Ravens, and the outage lasted thirty-four minutes. Ten minutes after the outage began, Oreo seized an opportunity, tweeting a simple picture of a solitary Oreo with the tagline "You Can Still Dunk in the Dark" and a tweet that read, "Power out? No problem."

Thirty-four minutes was all it took for Oreo to deliver one of the most buzz-worthy advertisements of the day. Within the hour, the tweet was retweeted 10,000 times.[5] On top of that, within minutes, Oreo's Twitter following grew by 8,000, the post got 20,000 likes on Facebook, and Oreo's Instagram following grew from 2,000 to 36,000.[6]

The audience reaction was incredible, making advertising executives scratch their heads in wonder at the tweet, which was developed and approved in minutes, when compared to Oreo's multi-million-dollar Super Bowl ad. It was a successful real-time marketing event that no one could have anticipated, but somehow Oreo executives and their advertising team did. The brand crafted a strategy to respond, if need be, during the Super Bowl. The opportunity presented itself in the form of a blackout, and Oreo and company responded in a big way. How did they do it?

1. They talked about the audience members. ("You Can Still Dunk in the Dark.")
2. Oreo spoke in detail. ("Power out? No problem.")
3. They created a meaningful dialogue that resonated with their audience.
4. Finally, Oreo told a story, a relevant story, though ever so short, and thousands of individuals responded.

Participating in the Conversation

Oreo, by simply listening and paying attention to what the conversation was about (the blackout at the Super Bowl), was able to jump into the conversation at the molecular level. Think in terms of where on the molecular level you are in participating in the conversation, whatever the conversation may be. When you figure out where your customers are, you can participate live on social media, through a blog, or some other type of media like a magazine. You can produce content and hope for a response, or listen on social media and then try to lead or participate in the conversation in real time.

Working at the molecular level on social media is known as participating in "micro-conversations." Macro-conversations like how to save for retirement, for example, get disrupted by micro-conversations about why the stock market crashed 10 percent that week. Suddenly, the macro-conversation about saving for the long term gets disrupted by micro-conversations about what to do in the short term.

In response, a financial advisor, can push out content in real time to their clients to provide reassurances that they're in good hands—content that says, "Hey, we've done research and we feel this drop in the market was precipitated by electronic trading, not fundamentals. If you're going to stay fully invested in the market, here are some tips on protecting your portfolio in the short term, without taking your eye off your long-term goals." Being relevant on a molecular level is addressing the needs of customers, not just with broad, "evergreen" topics, but those beneath the surface that are timely and in the moment.

The Road to Irrelevance: Common Mistakes Marketers Make

Often, in the attempt to be more relevant, marketers can make mistakes that actually make them irrelevant:

- Making the information your audience members need hard to find. Investors with questions go to investment websites, but if they have a question about 401k plans or how to budget their Social Security checks, are those "molecular" topics easy to find?
- Being afraid to go niche and casting too wide a net (talking too broadly), thereby alienating your audience.

- Using jargon or slang and making members of your audience feel left out or confused.
- Sounding like a cheerleader for your company.
- Talking about yourself. Developing promotional copy cloaked as content.

An important one here is leaving out the jargon and speaking human. If you're writing a blog for a relationship therapy practice, avoid phrases like, "After performing an extensive gap analysis, it was conclusive that the synergies between the subjects were present at the onset and will continue to exist in the future" when what you're really trying to say is, "After several months of intense counseling, the couple realized the love that brought them together is the same love that will keep them together."

Remember: No matter how tempting it is to show off your academic prowess, there is no substitute for meaningful prose. Don't be so fact-focused that you forget to make a personal connection.

An "Audience" Is Still One Person at a Time

In the discussion so far, you've learned that each person is an audience in and of themselves, which leads to the question: How can they all be reached effectively when companies, in most cases, have an extremely diverse audience? It all goes back to the strategy discussion. It's an exercise with your firm in trying to figure out who they're talking to plus the old argument about not selling a man a camera but showing him how to use it.

Imagine you're a camera company and you're tasked with starting a blog targeting an audience of both professional and amateur photographers. You're tasked with selling everything to everyone. Your company sells simple point-and-shoot cameras to the amateurs and elaborate DSLRs to the pros.

In this scenario, you have to think of each person (the typical amateur or the typical pro) as an audience of one, entirely unto themselves. They have a general sense of what they'd like to do, maybe know a few different techniques, and use their cameras in unique ways. How will you organize the information in your strategy to address their pain points and answer their questions? And how will you make this information easy for them to find?

Information must be organized in a way that addresses these needs as well as engages your audience members. You're about to jump into a macro-conversation that has already started. When you jump in, what is your unique contribution to the conversation that will make individual photographers stop and take notice? As some point, you need to choose words on a molecular level—meaning you have to find information that's relevant and important to each member of the audience and organized in a way that's easy for them to find it. When a person feels confident that you're able to solve a problem or pain point and answers are easy to find through your channel, you've become a resource for them. Don't underestimate the branding power that means for you. They may not use your services now, but when your blog or channel is elevated to a "utility" for someone, they come back time and time again, and likely share what they find with others.

. . . .

WebMD Magazine: A Case Study

One of the more brilliant examples of a targeted, relevant content marketing strategy is *WebMD Magazine.* From inception, WebMD recognized themselves as a lifestyle brand with all the articles pertaining to health.

As an unwitting member of their target audience, you've likely found yourself at the doctor's office and noticed a stack of WebMD magazines, adorned with a celebrity on the cover and an article related to pop culture. The information is relevant—grabbing an audience who's taking care of their health. And it just so happens that Oprah, or some other equally popular celebrity, is on the cover talking about her secrets to eating healthy and living right.

WebMD Magazine's appeal lies in the fact that it's a catch-all for a multitude of personalities, but the topic remains the same: preventative maintenance (i.e., lifestyle choices). And it lends itself to mostly general practitioners' offices—the doctors everyone is seeing for annual physicals and checkups. On top of that, once you have the hard copy in your hands, you can subscribe to the digital copy, which is delivered right to your inbox.

WebMD knows their audience and uses qualitative and quantitative research to find the relevant topics of interest to a vast array of audience members. In the early years of modern content marketing, quantitative data was hard to come by. Ten years ago, there were no "listening" tools of much value. Companies did all the "listening" the old-fashioned way—by trolling message boards, social media, cable news networks, or private news channels. Businesses had to keep their "ear to the ground." Of course, in many respects, those tried and true "qualitative" methods still work. But by adding the quantitative analysis (using data to guide your content) to spur new ideas, entities like WebMD get the one-two punch a content marketing strategy needs.

Any industry can learn a great deal from the success of *WebMD Magazine* in reaching their target audiences with relevant, interesting topics. One of first things you should do is make sure you hire people who specialize in what you do and can convey that knowledge in an effective and entertaining way. In other words, don't hire a brick layer to paint a house. If you're a medical supplies brand, then be sure you hire writers who have subject matter expertise in the medical field. It's a tough subject. If you are WebMD, you don't want to run something that is trite or take the risk of being inaccurate.

The circle of content relevancy begins with SEO. Once you have the keywords, you have to craft an article that doesn't sound like everything else out there. To do that, you need to be someone who knows what's going on in the industry, something that WebMD does very well.

For example, the latest issues included:

- Viola Davis speaking about her own childhood hunger and how now she works to eradicate the problem of children's hunger.
- Sharon Stone explaining her passion and advocacy on behalf of HIV and AIDS.
- Zoe Saldana offering tips for health care and raising a family.
- Jim Gaffigan and his wife, Jeannie Gaffigan, discussing their life while she underwent treatment for a brain stem tumor.

They also included relevant content such as:

- Ten healthy habits in the new year.
- Ways to curb anxiety.
- PTSD.
- Lupus.
- Healthy recipes.

WebMD Magazine is listening well, collecting the necessary data, and reaching their audience effectively through both print and digital media.

Super Molecular: A Final Thought

In a previous life, I taught investment seminars. One day, sometime in 2004, a student of mine, a retired gentleman from Texas, with $500,000 in his retirement account, pulled me aside and said, "I want to put all my money in Ford. I worked there my whole life, and I want to buy American!"

I'm not a financial adviser, and I'm sure most financial advisers would shudder at this idea. Don't put all your eggs in one basket, right? But I knew better. I took the time to explain to him how he could not only do this but protect his investment entirely. "Buy all the stock you can afford but leave enough to buy puts on the whole position," I told him. (A put is a form of "insurance" that protects a stock against price declines.)

Later that year, the stock got cut in half, and yes, his investment got cut in half, too. However, his puts increased as much, completely offsetting the loss in the stock, so he came out unscathed. He would have lost half his life savings if he'd invested directly, but he ended up losing just a few thousand on the cost of the protection.

The success of this story can be credited to pure content marketing at the conversational level. My student came in from the company blog, which he discovered online. He attended a free event where he learned the basics of options. He paid for a seminar, which he was able to attend multiple times to learn something that he didn't already know. When he was ready, he had a micro-conversation with me personally, which ended up saving him from losing nearly $250,000. He shared his experience with others, and got friends and family involved in the seminar as well.

I realize that you may not be able to have this type of molecular conversation in person with each customer. And neither could I. But his success, and the success of the company I worked for at the time, was based entirely on the back of a thoughtful content marketing strategy that became a relevant conversation on a molecular level.

The point is, your content strategy doesn't have to stop with a blog or social media channel. This was a series of content channels strung together strategically, with conversation-based marketing at each level. The path to purchase for him took him through three channels before he became a customer. But the lifetime value of this person was far greater as he recommended us to the many people he brought in after he became a brand ambassador.

Icebreaker

Can you build a business entirely by having a relevant conversation on a molecular level, from information that began as content strategy?

In his book, *Content Inc.*, Joe Pulizzi explains how to create and execute a content marketing strategy before building the product. Its premise basically states you build an audience first with good, relevant content. Then give them a reason to buy from you. For this exercise, challenge yourself to think about how you might attack a content strategy for your product or business if all you had was content. How deep (molecular) would you go to cultivate a relationship with your brand ambassadors?

The audience is built around a pain point. In my case, one of the pain points for the seminars was people were losing money in the market. The audience was built and retained by the company's blog at the center of a content marketing strategy that used several content channels that provided relevant, useful, knowledge-based articles and seminars.

Now, as an exercise, rethink your strategy right now along these lines:

1. Build an audience around a pain point. What is the pain point in *your* industry that is happening right now? If you aren't sure, stop and listen carefully before moving to the next step.

2. How can you address, answer, or solve the problem of the pain point in a relevant, unique, and useful way? Think about how to use at least one of your channels as a means of a "one to many" conversation, as if it were one to one, with you sharing your knowledge.

3. What channel(s) will best reach your audience most effectively? A blog, a newsletter, Facebook posts, emails, articles on a webpage, seminars, or a combination of two or more?

Get your relevant conversation going at the molecular level, build your following, and then introduce what you have to offer as you build your business.

CHAPTER 6

Open Up and Listen

D on't interrupt me!

How many times did you hear that as a kid? (I certainly did.) As adults we think it every time we get cut off by someone else at the end of a sentence before we have a chance finish our thought. To be a good conversationalist, you have to be a good listener. Yes, your brand has something to say, but if you're inwardly focused on the sale, and not outwardly focused on the information needs of the customer, you're not helping them.

How do you know what to write about each time you set out to write a blog, shoot a video, or record a podcast? To start, take a step back. Your audience is already engaged in a conversation with others. Of course, you have subject matter expertise that will guide your content iteration, but while they're talking, it pays to listen to your audience to gain insight into what makes them tick. In addition to what you already know, what are their pain points? Their needs? Or more specifically, what do they need from *you*? How can you take care of those needs right now, so they feel connected and attuned to you? What information can you provide in the moment?

Setting up a listening regimen is a critical part of the content ideation process, and essentially takes the form of three steps.

A relationship exists between you and your audience—one that needs to be cultivated through trust and understanding. Your audience is not merely a group, but a collection of individuals, each unique with varied thoughts, beliefs, passions, and ideologies. Your audience is not just a target you're trying to make money from, but individuals with whom you're trying to connect and have a conversation—between two or more individuals, not a one-sided lecture with no input from them.

If you approach every conversation from a standpoint of listening, you can gain greater understanding as well as the connection you seek with your audience. It's just like life. Think about how much more successful you would be in love and life if you became a better listener. Listening validates the other person. And validation builds trust and advocacy. When you listen more than you speak to your children, your partner, your friends, and your mentors, you gain a special advantage in virtually every conversation.

Naturally, the conversation should always begin with listening. If you're simply creating content for the sake of content, you become part of the noise that your audience is shutting out and turning off. Standing out as an individual, whether personally or professionally, requires you to listen with quiet resolve and speak at the right time to the ideal audience, with the right words, and the right tone. Knowing your audience and connecting with them is all about listening.

In their #SpeakBeautiful campaign, Dove collaborated with Twitter to change the way people talk about beauty on social media. After listening to their audience, Dove knew how to engage in what would be a successful campaign to reach their audience and make a positive change and create affinity for a traditional brand.

. . . .

Dove: A Case Study

In February 2015, Dove launched the #Speak Beautiful, campaign in conjunction with Twitter to coincide with Hollywood's biggest red-carpet event: the Academy Awards. The goal of the campaign was to change the conversation about beauty from judgmental to supportive and positive on social media.

The plan was simple. Through #Speak Beautiful Dove, a global beauty brand, struck an emotional chord by encouraging women to speak positively about themselves and others on social media. And there was no mention of soap—anywhere.

Dove was inspired to launch the campaign by their own research (they listened). The Dove research showed that "8 out of 10 women encounter negative comments on social media that critique women's looks while only nine percent of women admitted to posting negative comments on social media."[1] In addition, Dove's research revealed "four out of every five negative tweets about beauty and body image are written by women critiquing themselves."[2]

The campaign launched with Twitter on Oscar night in February 2015, with a thirty-second commercial. It immediately put the power directly in the hands of women to impact social media in a positive way—encouraging one another and expressing positive beauty images online. The Dove #SpeakBeautiful campaign used Twitter's latest technology to track the negative tweets regarding beauty and body image and allowed Dove to respond with positive tweets from self-esteem experts and social media. The goal: empower women with self-esteem and confidence.

Everyone joined in, including celebrities, spreading positive beauty messages across Twitter. #SpeakBeautiful quickly turned into a positive movement, changing the conversation regarding beauty and body image. Statistics showed these results:

- 2014: 5.3 million negative tweets regarding beauty/body image
- 2015: 3.4 million negative tweets regarding beauty/body image (a 36.8 percent reduction)
- From Oscar night 2014 to 2015, women posted 30 percent fewer negative tweets and 69 percent more positive tweets about themselves.
- #SpeakBeautiful was used more than 168,000 times and drove 800 million social media impressions.
- #SpeakBeautiful drove affinity for Dove up 17 percent.[3]

Who thinks soap is boring now?! The results of Dove's #SpeakBeautiful surpassed all expectations, increased brand awareness, and made social media a more positive place. Mission accomplished. And it started by listening effectively.

How to Listen Effectively

In personal communication, listening is a learned skill everyone needs to know. Likewise, in business, listening effectively is crucial to a successful content marketing strategy. If you don't know how to listen to your customers and your prospects, not only will you have difficulty reaching them, you'll have difficulty retaining them, too. Here are a few ideas.

Mine for What Your Customer Thinks

If you're stuck and need help finding your customers and what they're talking about, at some point, you'll want to quantify what's trending with the help of "listening tools" that mine for this information.

Such tools expedite this process, giving you automated ways of listening to the conversation in social media and quantify the data. These tools are commonly used by researchers and marketing and communications teams to understand what customers are saying, keep on top of the latest trends, and track what their competitors are doing. Listening tools automatically monitor consumer posts in different languages and various countries, providing a number of ways to help brands reach their audiences. You can first try using Google's free Keyword Planner and Google Trends, or go straight to something more powerful like BuzzSumo and Moz.

Social media listening tools seek out specific mentions on social media, identifying trending topics, and organizing customers' chatter and information. In addition, these tools can also spot leaders and influencers in your industry. There are a few popular tools as starting points:

- Hootsuite: Its old reputation as a convenient place to deploy your messaging across all your social media accounts shouldn't fool you. It's also a great social listening tool.

- Sprout Social: It allows you to listen to social conversations about topics as well as what consumers are saying, notifying you of all social media interactions in a single place while you monitor your competitors.
- Talkwalker: Since it gets its data from over 150 million websites and tracks conversation in about 190 languages from around the world, it deserves a seat at the table here.

When using these tools, don't forget to search for your brand name and all its variations (including alternate spellings and abbreviations), as well as your name and the names of other key team members. You'll also want to include any taglines, mottoes, messages, or slogans your brand uses along with keywords used in your industry.

When you use these tools, remember they aren't there to stroke your ego; they should be used to join conversations, interact and engage with those talking about your brand, your competition's brands, and fill gaps in your content to meet needs based on what is being discussed. Don't be sensitive if some posts are negative. Instead, listen and utilize as you would constructive criticism. Following up and interacting with negative and positive posts shows your humility and transparency, making you and your brand more human.

Go Where Your Customers Are Hanging Out

Turn your focus to where your customers are congregating. This doesn't mean going to your local coffeehouse, but rather find out where your customers are gathering online. Where are they hanging out on social media? Are they on Facebook, Twitter, Instagram, or LinkedIn?

If you're a B2B company, for example, you'll likely be trolling LinkedIn. If you're more B2C, such as a local ice cream shop or major retail chain, you're more likely to go to Facebook or Twitter to find your audience.

There are a number of great campaigns businesses have created as a result of listening to their audience and discovering "Hey, you know what? There's a whole section of our audience here or there. . . ." You might be a candy manufacturer who thought only children were eating your candy, only to discover on social media that you have an audience of nostalgic adults who loved your candy growing up. By listening, not only will you discover where to find your audience and what they want to talk about, but you'll also find out whom to talk to as well. Suddenly, you've uncovered some people interested in your products that you didn't even know existed.

By hanging out and listening, you can also find out who is doing the talking about your products or services. You also want to know if they are joining in a conversation started by someone else or if they are leading the conversations on social media. Once you know that, ask how you can make a contribution to those people. How can you help them or meet a need for them? And that's just the beginning.

Ask on Social Media

Get your customers involved by giving them some ownership in the content ideation process. Many, many, good topics have come from ideas the customers requested themselves on social channels. After all, if one customer is asking, there are probably many more who are out there seeking the same information and simply haven't taken the time to ask. Give it to them!

But beware of the caveat: You may not like what you hear. Sometimes this approach can spawn negative attacks that have nothing to do with content suggestions. Be ready to moderate the conversation and check your feeds regularly.

Survey for Customer Feedback

In truth, most successful businesses have a good idea of what their customers need, but they don't always know what their customers are talking about. Collecting customer feedback by survey is a qualitative form of listening that's less scientific than other methods, but it can be extremely effective when done correctly and inform your content marketing strategy.

Conducting a survey can be great, but before you know what the problem is, you may find the results are limited to a few responses or certain types of people who don't necessarily represent your entire audience demographic. This alone means surveys can exclude a majority of your customers right off the bat.

Another problem you could run into with surveys is there may not be a large enough response to provide anything meaningful. If you were expecting 100 respondents and only got five back, and they were who were all negative, you run the risk of assuming the worst and start globalizing what amounts to a small issue. When it comes to surveys, the best results are when enough people respond, and there's a balance of both positive and negative feedback that might prompt meaningful change.

• •

Tips for Writing an Effective Survey

- Keep it short. When the average attention span of a person today is eight seconds, most wouldn't fill out a survey that takes eight minutes.[4] Keep the survey less than ten questions max, which takes around five minutes to take—the length of time in which the average person spends taking a survey.[5]

- Front-load the most important questions. The average time a person spends on the first question of a survey is one minute; the remaining questions get less and less.[6] Because the first question receives the most thought, you're going to get the most accurate responses out of the first few. Put the "must have" questions that you value the most upfront, and park the "nice to haves" in the back.

- Offer an incentive (if you can). Some heavily regulated industries won't allow incentives to get feedback, but if you can, offer discounts and freebies that won't break you, but cost less than not having the information. You're more likely to get a higher response rate when you give 'em skin in the game.

- Don't sway the survey taker. If you're trying to get honest feedback, try not to drive the language that deliberately elicits the response you seek. Maybe you're trying to get a sense of which way to go in particular content strategy, such as offering free content or paid content. If you ask your audience what they'd rather have, the answer is obvious. Everyone loves free. But that shouldn't discourage you from charging for your content if it creates a more valued customer. "Would you be willing to pay for this content?" could be a better way to get what you're after.

• •

Data + Gut = Success

Whatever protocols you choose to use to listen to your audience, one thing is for sure: You simply can't extrapolate all the information you need from data alone (quantitative) or gut feeling and experience (qualitative). You need both.

If you approach marketing from gut instinct alone, you're going to be dead wrong if you don't take into account that you might be a part of the minority. If you like a product or an idea, or you use a product in a certain way, then you'll seek out others who are in agreement. If you ignore the data and only look for evidence to validate what you're already thinking, you're not getting the whole picture. And likewise, if you're only tracking data without the guidance of your subject matter expertise, you're reading data in a vacuum where you can make a lot of mistakes and miss opportunities.

The optimal method for content topic creation is what I call "policing the data." In other words, applying qualitative review on top of quantitative data. You can use the listening tools to pinpoint trending keywords and existing conversations in your niche, but you should apply your institutional knowledge of your industry to make final decisions for true relevancy. Just because a topic may find its way into the "trending" bucket of your search doesn't mean you should use it. The topic may be similar to what you're looking for, but not relevant to your niche. If it's not helpful for your purpose, then don't use it.

Points of View: Good Versus Bad

In general, people tend to be more outspoken when they have an unusually bad experience. When you're listening, this makes it harder to find those with good opinions, but it's possible.

In fact, all you have to do is ask. If you're listening well, people, particularly on social media, give a lot of thumbs up and thumbs down. On most social media sites, there's some sort of "Like" system that can give you a sense if your content is resonating.

People truly do, even if only in a small way, use these methods to give you a sense of their likes or dislikes. If someone likes what you're saying, they tend to share it on social media. The more your content is being shared, the more likely the audience is getting something from it, making it a positive experience and projecting a good opinion. The less your content is being shared can mean many things, among them:

1. You haven't been pushing content out long enough to have built an audience that cares enough to respond.
2. You need to revisit your distribution/channel strategy.
3. It's just not that good.

You don't want to discount any one of these reasons, but if your content isn't being shared or you get negative comments, be careful jumping to conclusions that the majority didn't like it. You may be getting negative feedback from only a limited number of your audience. No matter the numbers you're analyzing—100 shares, ten shares, or one share, doesn't matter—you have to consider how much time and effort you put into your content marketing and whether or not you have done it correctly.

Keeping Points of View Positive

You may be wondering if there is anything you can do to keep your customers' points of view positive. First of all, what point of view are you talking about? Are you discussing the point of view of your company or the point of view of your customers? What is the point you want to keep positive? Are you trying to maintain a positive point of view of yourself as an industry expert or trying to keep customers' point of view positive about your customer service?

Generally speaking, you're probably most concerned with keeping your clients' points of view positive. How do you keep your customers feeling positive about you and your brand? At first glance you may think classic customer service or possible content value or, depending on your business, your product's usefulness and longevity. But there is so much more to consider in maintaining a positive point of view from your customers in relation to your business.

- Keeping open an honest, forthright conversation.
- Being vulnerable.
- Admitting you're not perfect.
- Owning your mistakes.

Traditionally companies have been tight-lipped, never vulnerable, always presenting the perfect image, and never admitting to making a mistake. But this is changing, with the credit for the shift due in large part to millennials. Millennials are expecting to have a conversation with brands, which means more damage is done when a company fails to show their vulnerability, humility, and humanity. You cannot try to be perfect all the time to everyone because you fear a lawsuit or a tarnished reputation.

Will an MBA Help You Listen?

The answer, of course, is it depends. Each of those individuals can certainly help you with general-purpose content marketing, but think about it, you're not likely going to need an MBA to market your flower shop unless you're going to produce content about the science of growing flowers. If, on the other hand, you're in a niche market (financial, legal, medical, or engineering), then these professionals may help you listen and start a conversation with your audience.

None of this means you need an MBA. Though it's great to get as much education as you can, it will not necessarily make you better at content marketing. To be a good content marketer, you need to have natural insight into the human condition and understand how to be a good listener.

To succeed in your industry, whatever it is, you do need a certain level of expertise. But remember: Expertise does not come in a few months, or immediately following college graduation. Expertise is a product of years in an industry. And that means you need professionals on your team who have expert insight into the content you're producing and the conversations you're hoping to have with your audience.

My firm is grounded in the financial industry, and because it is, I know journalists who spend years writing about fiscal and economic issues. We hire those former journalists because it's mandatory our content writers have a solid financial background to write about investments. We don't consider those who claim to be good writers with no background in the industry. Why? Because a good writer with no financial expertise cannot produce insightful and informative content to educate our audience on investments.

How to Speak the Way Your Customer Wants to Be Spoken To

In the real world, we use our tone of voice and our body language to convey meaning. When you're listening and trying to have a meaningful conversation with someone and relate to them, you often imitate their body language. It is known as mirroring in the world of psychology, and it has proven to be a powerful tool in building rapport and understanding. Mirroring is instinctive, like smiling when the person you're talking to smiles or crossing your arms when the individual crosses their arms.

Mirroring facial expressions and body language communicates the message that you're alike—you're in agreement with the others in the conversation. This helps people feel secure in your presence as it builds trust and understanding. The synchronous behavior of mirroring creates confidence and camaraderie. It shows you're removing the mask and being real with those in the conversation.

Mirroring extends beyond facial expressions and body language into voices, tones, and accents. For example, if someone is speaking to you in a loud voice, you may speak to them in the same way, mirroring their tone. Everyone tends to take on the mannerisms of those they are communicating with. It's intuitive and instinctual. Think about how you tend to take on the tones and accents of those you're speaking to when you travel.

You also mirror voice, accents, and tone when you're trying to ingratiate yourself to another, attempting to accomplish a task or goal. If someone is speaking in a specific way, there will be a certain amount of slang in the dialogue. Younger generations will use words and colloquialisms that seem unconventional to them. In the same way, if you're speaking to an organization at the professional level, you'll encounter more formal speech, less slang, more neutral language—professional language.

To understand people, you have to be a good listener. You should always be listening for verbal cues and looking for non-verbal cues. You can gain valuable information from both, especially verbal cues. As you listen, ask these questions:

- Are they using exaggerated words?
- Are they using slang?
- Are they having a youthful conversation?
- Are they telling jokes?
- What's the predominant conversation?

Targeted marketing should happen on the platform of the user's choice—not yours. We don't target customers on Snapchat the same way we target customers through print media. Those are different user bases, and as such our conversation with them needs to have the appropriate voice.

When people are engaged in these group conversations, whether in person or responding to social media in your industry, how are they doing it? It really is all about ingratiating yourself with the audience by analyzing both the spoken word and the written word. You have to listen carefully if you want to join the conversation and communicate effectively.

You can't always see the non-verbal clues, but, when you can, pay close attention because they reveal a great deal about people. Look at how they look at you and examine their body language.

Mirroring body language, facial expressions, voice, and tone can help you build understanding and develop trust. You can establish a connection and communicate better when you mirror your audience, from body language to facial expressions to tone of voice to pace of speech. You will make them feel they like you when you reflect their mannerisms and voice, developing the rapport you seek.

What They Want Versus What They Really Want

Considerable research suggests that consumers don't actually know what they want. There are two schools of thought here. The first is the philosophy embodied by

Steve Jobs, who famously said, "A lot of times, people don't know what they want until you show it to them."[7] Jobs operated on the notion that customers truly don't know what they want, and so Apple showed them—and he did so successfully.

Same with rock and roll. Before the Beatles's first appearance on *The Ed Sullivan Show* in 1964, nobody had sounded like them before. Then it was Led Zeppelin in the '70s, U2 in the '80s, and Nirvana in the '90s. All pioneers with virtually no "data" in today's conventional sense to suggest each of their unique sound would be successful. If all the bands that came after Elvis thought they should sound like Elvis because that's what the data said worked, rock and roll wouldn't have evolved. (I shudder to even think it.)

The second philosophy is the camp that follows the evolving pattern to achieve success. There are a million copycat bands that do very well following the model of the current precedent in their industry. Great success can be awarded to those who can replicate the successful model of the day very, very well. So suddenly, U2 becomes the greatest sound of the day, and you hear a lot of bands that sound a little bit like U2 and gain some measure of success, until the next band comes out in five or ten years with a unique new sound. The point is, you've got people who jump on the bandwagon of whatever is trending at the moment and give the consumers what they want, and you have the unique individuals who are developing the industry in creative and distinctive ways.

Now, that doesn't really answer the question "How do you tell the difference?" but it does set the stage. In order to answer the question in your industry, try it both ways. Test the waters. Dare to be different to get noticed, but always be relevant. You can easily quantify the results. In content marketing, whatever you do to gauge what your customers want to hear and what they don't want to hear, should provide you a good sense of what is going on in the conversations and what they want to hear. If you do try something new, stick with it for a little while. Consumers might not like it at first, but that doesn't mean they won't ever like it or it's not going to take hold. You can't change an entire strategy based on one or two comments, or one or two social media posts, or any similar small response. If some*one* doesn't like what you said, it doesn't mean it's not going to work. You've got to give it some time to play out.

That is the big different between content marketing and traditional marketing. In traditional marketing, if you create a thirty-second commercial and you don't get the million hits you thought you would, you might have time to change your campaign and do something else. In content marketing, you've got to stick with it a little longer because you'll earn trust over time. You're not going to earn trust in thirty seconds. It's going to take a while for people to respond to your attempts at reaching out to them. They don't trust you yet. You've just entered the conversation, and you have to give them time to listen to you as you become part of the conversation, listen, and eventually earn their trust.

Icebreaker

At the beginning of this chapter, you learned to not interrupt if the audience is talking. Even if the talk is negative, listen. You can learn a great deal by listening to what they are saying, negative or positive.

Right now, take the time to do some research, listening to the talk in the industry, among your customers, and among your prospects. Once your initial research is done, answer these questions honestly as you prepare to move into Chapter 7, where you'll learn how to start a conversation with your content:

1. Listen to the conversations. What is being said?
2. What do customers and prospects need right now?
3. What are the topics they want to hear about (not the topics you want to talk about)?
4. What is being said about your brand (the good and the bad)?
5. What are the audience's pain points?
6. How can you take care of their needs right now, making them feel connected to you?

CHAPTER 7

Start the Conversation

Early on in this book, we talked about the "handshake moment," and in this chapter, we'll unwrap that concept further. After all the planning, segmenting, and analyzing, the channel strategy is in place, and at some point, you have to start the conversation. But, just how do you get noticed? This chapter addresses how to gain the attention of the audience so you're not just part of the noise.

It's no longer a question of whether you should insert yourself into the world of content marketing. It's a matter of when you are going to start talking and what you are going to say. What is your handshake moment? What is your unique value proposition to the audience?

This chapter is all about deciding what you are going to say. Everything, we've discussed so far—being humble, storied, and relevant—has been leading up to this point. You still have to come up with memorable content that's interesting and unique. You need to plan your handshake moment.

Remember What You've Learned So Far

Your target audience, the ones you are attempting to start the conversation with, only care about themselves when they read your content. They are looking to solve a problem immediately or looking for incremental knowledge they didn't already have about your area of expertise. Designing a story that helps someone is not peddling; it's your content marketing obligation. You're taking action to help someone.

If you had the time, you'd ask every audience member individually about themselves. But because that's not the role of content, you need to frame an answer to a question you know your audience has that is relevant to your industry and the audience but that isn't about you or your product.

For example, if you're in the travel business, instead of a blog post titled "How to Get Your Next Vacation at Half the Price" (you-focused), you might opt for something like "Discount Travel: Smart Vacation Hacks to Live Like a King at a Pauper's Price" (uses a smart keyword phrase with a clever, problem-solving angle). If you're a wine distributor, don't be tempted to write and distribute a blog titled "Five Ways to Save on Wine." Try writing instead "Sour Grapes? Five Tips for Spotting a Bad Wine Before Uncorking It."

Remember that storytelling is about a narrative. So it's critical to remember that when you tell your story, the reader is the hero. And the hero is living in an unfolding story that you want to join and be an integral part. Every experience has a story, and when you start a conversation, you need to tap into the hero's story to drive him or her ultimately to action.

As you begin any conversation, you must speak the language of the channel. Social media has colloquialisms appropriate for each channel and often only that channel. LinkedIn sounds different than Twitter; Snapchat sounds different than Facebook; and so on.

Always in the back of your mind should be the question "What's the *big idea?*" Before you embark on any content creation, you must decide what you're going to write about. Then, as you move forward, ask these questions:

1. Why did you start this?
2. What was the broad subject matter you wanted to cover?
3. What makes you the industry leader?
4. Why should people listen?

Tips for Starting a Conversation

As always, when starting a conversation, you lead with the audience member, not with you. Once your id is out of the way, then you can start the conversation.

Find the Right Angles

Don't be a "me, too" marketer by writing about the same topics you and everyone else can find all over the place. Be a thought leader and dig to discover the unobvious. Sometimes, this might be incremental knowledge about topics your reader didn't realize they wanted and needed to know. Think of yourself as an entrepreneur in the problem-solving business. Then, when your customers need you, your expertise, or your products and services, they come to you because you're the voice of authority. In the downtime, when they aren't seeking you out to meet their needs, you're still interacting with them with your always-on content marketing. Let your competition fight for the bottom with the next article about "Five Reasons to Do This or That." Figure out the right angle—the one that hasn't been talked about—and don't be afraid to go there. Your audience will appreciate that you did.

Go Deep

Make 'em laugh, cry, get angry, cringe, hope, dream, and so forth. Once you've figured out the topic you want to write about, you have to make it memorable. Connect with your audience on an emotional level, and they'll not only share it, but they'll stick around for more from you. Today, brand ambassadors are won and lost at the content level. Make them love you, and they'll talk about you forever.

Craft Your Headlines

There's a "function over form" debate among content marketers. Are you writing for bots or humans? If you write headlines that are keyword rich, you'll help your search engine results. But just slapping up keywords and adding "Ten Tips" in front of them could lead to awkward headlines devoid of rhythm and difficult to remember. And ultimately, you'll soon be forgotten— the very minute the reader leaves your article. It's worth putting some time into thinking through your headlines. As marketing pioneer David Ogilvy said, "On average, five times as many people read the headline as they do the copy. When you've written your headline, you've spent eighty cents out of your dollar."[1]

• •

Ten Tips for Clear, Clever (and Effective) Headlines

1. You're a thought leader and a problem-solver. Most people looking for your information will find you because they're looking to solve a problem. Write your headlines with that in mind.

2. Sometimes to make both bots and humans happy, you can use colons to split up the keyword from the prose (for example, "Writing Headlines: Why Yours Suck and How to Fix Them").

3. Pick simple words. Don't drop *pedantic* when the majority of people say *overthinking*. Use clean, simple language that everybody can understand.

4. Target keywords with high search volumes. (Use Moz Keyword Explorer or Google AdWords Keyword Planner to start finding them.)

5. Numbers work (e.g., "Seven Reasons to . . .", "Forty-five Places You Must Visit Before You Marry"). Use odd numbers for higher click-through rates.

6. Ask a question in your title. It could be a bizarre question or simply one that arouses curiosity.

7. Say something cute, clever, or funny. If you can make 'em smile, you've nailed it.

8. Negatives can be positive (e.g., "These Three Bad Sitting Habits Are Killing You").

9. Avoid clichés. (This should apply to all your content!)

10. Be concise: Eight to twelve words tends to be the consensus, but not more than seventy characters, as that would cut you off of search engine results.

Writing Content Made Easy: Ask Three Questions

To earn attention, we discussed that you should have useful, memorable, and sharable content. Three questions at the core of a successful content creation process for your content marketing strategy are:

1. What does your target audience need to know about right now? In other words, what is a relevant, useful (and trending) topic at the moment?
2. What's the right angle? That is, how can you talk about the topic in a way that hasn't already been talked about?
3. What's the punchline? What do you want them to do?

Imagine you're writing content for a financial brokerage firm and you're tasked with educating active investors on how to protect their portfolios against market swoons. This is a familiar topic for most people with a long-term portfolio, and one that has been written about ad nauseam. How would you approach this differently using the three questions above?

My firm was faced with this task when one of our clients asked us to write a series of articles on the subject of portfolio protection. Simple enough on the surface. But you would find no shortage of articles written about a subject such as that. Not wanting our client to sound like a me-too firm and get lost in the crowd, we focused on the tools and the market conditions themselves. In an article entitled "Bear Market Radar Detector," we focused on how to identify toppy markets that might be ripe for a fall. Oh, and it just so happened that our client had tools (of course) that the investor could use.

By simply answering the three content questions beforehand, we effectively solved for a small hurdle:

1. *What does your audience need to know about right now?*

Answer: Portfolio protection tips.

2. *What's the right angle?*

Answer: How individual investors can identify the warning signs a bear market is near as part of an overall portfolio strategy.

3. *What's the punchline?*

Answer: How to use the broker's unique set of online tools to effectively accomplish this without actually selling the tools.

As with any article, you're tying the information needs of the client with the marketing objective (in this case, introduce the tools), and it's a win-win for the investor and the broker.

Beyond the Headlines

Outside of the headline and substance of the article, there are a few rules of thumb to keep in mind when before you write a single word.

Don't bury the thesis. Tell them what you're going to tell them upfront. People's attention spans are short. If you only have thirty seconds to grab someone's attention, don't take sixty seconds to get to the point. Once you grab their attention, avoid colorful language that can distract.

Know your stuff. If you're selling paint, you better know a thing or two about painting. This may sound obvious, but even if you know your industry cold, be sure your content team isn't green. Your audience is looking to you for thought leadership and guidance, so you need to know your topic cold. Consider influencers to help with this (externally or internally). (More on this in Chapter 9.)

Hire writers who know your stuff. If you don't have the time to write your own material, hire specialists, not just writers who claim they can write on any subject. Two mistakes are most often made here: hiring cheap writers or hiring writers who write about any topic, particularly those who don't specialize in your industry. You get what you pay for, so if you're in a field that requires specialized knowledge, you may need to pony up for experienced, skilled writers in your industry.

Create an "editorial board." Outside writers should be expected to deliver good ideas regularly. This is a huge benefit that saves you time and money. You're not just paying writers for words on a page. You're also paying them for ideas, making them a part of the ideation process for topics.

Big Ideas for Longer Conversations

There are several types of content that truly grab an audience's attention. And those types of content are founded in capturing people's attention in an engaging way; providing them with useful, usable information; and positively influencing their thoughts about your brand.[2] Most attention-getting content can be used in various forms on multiple channels.

Content that addresses trending information delivers needed guidance on changing circumstances that are affecting your audience from you, the expert in the industry. Whether the changes are evolving slowly or occurring rapidly, your content should present solutions for your audience in relevant and supportive ways.

Another popular approach that captivates audiences is content that explains how to accomplish some task, activity, goal, or result. This type of content must be relevant, delivering information critical to success, for the audience and appear on a channel where the topic is already a part of the ongoing conversation.

Do Something Totally Unexpected

Totally unexpected content is content developed with the intention of going viral and building an audience quickly. Touch a nerve, funny or emotional. Keep in mind that humor is nearly always a winning formula. Videos seem to work well in this format. A few examples are: The Dollar Shave Club's "Our Blades are F***ing

Great" viral video, the Blend-it video series, and the TD Bank #TDThanksYou campaign.

• •

TD Bank: A Case Study

In 2014, TD Bank launched #TDThanksYou, and proceeded to give money and gifts to thank randomly selected customers at TD Bank "ATMs" (Automatic Thanking Machines). TD Bank hired a small content marketing agency to film the customers' reactions when they pulled a gift from the ATM. A single mom of two was the recipient of a trip to Disneyland and savings accounts for her kids, and another mom got airfare to Trinidad to visit her cancer-stricken daughter.[3] The videos went viral.

The #TDThanksYou campaign didn't stop there, as employees gave twenty dollars to every customer at banks or via direct deposit to say thank you. TD Bank continues the campaign every year as an annual event.

The viral video was viewed 5.2 million times in the first week, increased TD Bank's brand awareness by 26 percent, and became the most viewed in Canada for 2014.[4] TD Bank, a mammoth financial institution, suddenly became local, relatable, and surprisingly human.

• •

Other companies have done well with the "totally unexpected" angle and used it quite effectively. Take the whimsical music video from Jordan Vineyard & Winery parodying the mega-hit song "Despacito" to promote their cabernet sauvignon. The video was so successful that Jordan Winery discovered their voice in the crowded wine space that kicked off their video content brand (jordanwinery.com/videos). Though the company doesn't disclose the numbers, since the channel was introduced, sales, social media engagement, visits, and earned media have all gone up.[5]

A word of caution is needed here: Unexpected content doesn't always last as long as you'd like. Once you've done it the first time, it's simply not sustainable. But if you're starting a new campaign or looking for a jolt in engagement, this is a positive strategy to consider to kickstart things. Once you've established your content brand to your audience, be ready to parlay your success into content that is more long term.

Go Niche

In other words, go where others haven't. What if you could not only talk about something in a way nobody else did, but you invented a content brand that specialized in that topic?

To find your niche, start by exploring and researching content experiments through the years. Why, for example, did *Saturday Night Live* resonate with its audience when it first aired in 1975? Simple: Lorne Michaels thought the then-young late-night baby boomer audience needed a departure from the traditional format of *The Tonight Show* starring Johnny Carson. He was right. They needed, and wanted, something irreverent and cynical that wasn't going to ever be on Carson's show. He sold the idea to NBC. He knew the language of the Boomers, and the platform he developed for live, irreverent comedy was the perfect content channel. It was a niche that hadn't been capitalized yet because others feared breaking from the status quo.

In the world of content marketing, *thinkMoney* magazine that T3 Custom created for TD Ameritrade was not only unexpected, it was irreverent. The magazine targeted hyperactive online traders and gave this very niche audience something to connect offline with the brand. Not only that, it gave them the opportunity to learn new, tradable ideas, and laugh while doing it. Though online trading hit critical mass nearly a decade earlier, by 2007, no other financial brand had seen or capitalized on the opportunity. Most had only been interested in carving out marketing budgets for the greatest audience (buy and hold investors) rather than nurturing their smallest, most valuable audience (hyperactive traders) who often generate vastly more revenue than the average investor client.

And it worked. After reading *thinkMoney*, traders traded more, opened new accounts, consolidated old ones, and best of all, shared the information with their trading friends, who migrated to TD Ameritrade and did the same. The magazine became a cult hit, and its loyal readers became loyal customers. It was truly a differentiator.

Another outstanding example is the Content Marketing Institute. In 2009, Joe Pulizzi founded the Content Marketing Institute with a smart idea: build a business using only content marketing. It was a huge risk at the time.

His business concept was to target the fledgling content marketing industry with a new type of education firm. The plan: First, using a blog, build an audience of marketers entirely on content from other influential marketers eager for the exposure. Then develop a product this audience would not only want but come to need—an annual conference for showcasing content marketing best practices by other industry experts and influencers. Throw in a well-written, well-designed magazine, some limited, lucrative sponsorships, and—*voila!*—you have a recipe for success, all built on the back of content marketing itself.

There are many other examples of successfully going niche. It's worth the time and research to see if this method can help you start the conversation.

Five Wrong Ways to Start a Conversation

For all the ways we've mentioned for starting a successful conversation with your target audience, it's worth mentioning a few that you need to avoid. Although it's been said that even bad publicity can be good publicity, that's simply not always true in content marketing. Here are five surefire ways to stumble in starting the conversation.

1. You Don't Pay Attention

There's a great scene from Woody Allen's classic *Play It Again, Sam*. Woody Allen's character (Allan) is in an art museum standing next to a woman with whom he's trying to strike up a conversation. The woman (Museum Girl) is admiring a painting when this conversation ensues.

Allan: That's quite a lovely Jackson Pollock, isn't it?

Museum Girl: Yes, it is.

Allan: What does it say to you?

Museum Girl: It restates the negativeness of the universe. The hideous lonely emptiness of existence. Nothingness. The predicament of Man forced to live in a barren, Godless eternity, like a tiny flame flickering in an immense void with nothing but waste, horror, and degradation, forming a useless bleak straitjacket in a black absurd cosmos.

Allan: What are you doing Saturday night?

Museum Girl: Committing suicide.

Allan: What about Friday night?[6]

It seems Allan starts the conversation pretty well, using an object of shared interest (the painting) to kick things off. He even has a good follow-up question ("What does it say to you?"). However, as the rest of the conversation shows, he blows it in the end because he's obviously not paying attention to what she's saying.

In content marketing, once you get a conversation started, your job isn't over. In fact, it has only begun. You have to focus and listen to what the potential customer is saying during the conversation to fully understand their needs. Like so many inward-facing content marketing flops, in the scene, Woody Allen's character is so focused on his own needs (essentially selling himself as a product to a highly desirable customer) that he pays no attention to anything she's actually telling him. His desired end overtakes his ability to listen. Don't make his mistake. Don't blow it. Pay attention to what your potential customers are saying.

2. You Talk About Yourself, Not Your Customer

Nobody wants to listen to someone drone on about how great they are. Yet, throughout the decades, acceptable advertising copy has been what amounts to descriptions of a product's features and benefits, with a nod to what it will do to enrich consumers' lives. This is not cool if you're producing content that's doing the very same thing, however.

Here's a quick test to determine whether you're talking too much about yourself. Randomly pick some content you've already produced and count the number of times you mention your company's name or your product's name. Once or twice may be okay, depending on context, but any more than that, and you need to check your ego at the door because you have a problem.

A successful content marketing strategy turns traditional advertising on its head and asks customers to consider what they need, only then bringing up what the company offers to meet those exact needs. Do you have a tool that will solve your customer's problem?

Great news. Talk about the situation that inspired the need for the tool—the same pain points your customer is experiencing—then talk about the solution. A screenshot of your solution in action as part of the educational experience would deliver greater value than you boasting about how great you are for having developed it.

A lesson from the seminal 1930s book by Dale Carnegie, *How to Win Friends and Influence People,* still holds true eighty years later. You tend to make the best impression when you focus on the other person, not yourself.

Conversation starters are not unlike those you use on first dates as you're getting to know someone, questions like "What makes you laugh the hardest?" and "What is something I wouldn't guess about you?" Except, here, instead of asking questions while trying to get to know the other person, you're making assumptions based on the research you've done on your potential audience, about what they want to hear. You may not be asking any icebreaking questions in your handshake moments. You need to think of ways to make the conversation about your audience and their needs, not about you, your brand, or your product.

3. You Bring Up the Sale Too Early

Some companies have the wrong idea about content marketing. They create a YouTube video to park their TV ads or promote their product in an online blog, and immediately expect the proverbial phone to start ringing off the hook. And that approach might work for billboards selling fifty-cent burgers to hungry drivers, but it's definitely not a handshake moment.

It's hard for some marketers who are under pressure to produce immediate return on investment (ROI) to grapple with the longer sales cycle of content marketing. It requires more patience than putting up a billboard and quickly seeing those hungry drivers line up at your drive-thru window. The ultimate satisfaction of getting into a conversation with your audience is the personal relationship you can build with your customers and the ability you have to address different types of customers who need unique solutions from your company.

When advertising on a channel designed for visual storytelling like YouTube, and the story you're trying to tell the world is that you make cheap burgers, you are showing them you don't really value their time. This isn't a conversation; it's an interruption. Remember the golden rule of content marketing: Don't pitch. Teach.

4. You Offend Your Listener

Everyone can probably relate to committing a social faux pas by having said something that offended another person in the conversation. And though you probably never talked to that person again, you did survive the encounter. Businesses aren't so lucky.

A few years back, amid a spate of controversial police shootings across the U.S., Starbucks decided it could help bridge the racial divide by engaging in conversations about race at its coffee shops. It called the effort "Race Together," and asked its baristas to write the same phrase on its coffee cups and engage in conversations with their customers. Photos were snapped and pushed out on social media.

Arguably, Starbucks had the best intentions in mind, and certainly, they didn't intend for the campaign to sound condescending, but that's exactly how it was interpreted. With Howard Schultz, CEO and chairman of Starbucks, leading the charge, people felt as if they were being lectured by an individual who'd never experienced racism. Within forty-eight hours, the backlash produced more than 2.5 billion impressions, mostly spurred by outrage over the gesture.[7]

5. You Don't Do Your Research

If you've ever talked to a know-it-all who makes completely false statements, you understand the feeling of not trusting that person then, now, nor likely in the future. The same goes for your company's content when you spout falsities that could've been prevented with a little fact checking before your content is put out there for all to see.

A fact that seems difficult for marketers to understand is that if you're publishing content, then you have the same journalistic responsibilities as traditional media. Anyone and everyone producing content today are publishers. As such, everything your brand distributes out there could be consumed by the media landscape in equal proportion as traditional journalism. And as a result, there should be no less journalistic integrity.

Picking on Starbucks one more time (sorry, Howard), the company had to apologize in 2012 after inviting its Irish Twitter followers to "Show us what makes you proud to be British" as part of a Diamond Jubilee promotion.[8] Apparently, whoever put up the post didn't realize that Ireland is separate from Britain, and the company received threats from people who said they wouldn't come back to the coffee shop. Oops.

The lesson here is to fact check, fact check, fact check before you put a marketing plan forward. Know your audience and know the landscape. Starbucks failed in its Irish effort. But they learned from their mistake, and you can, too.

Icebreaker

Imagine you've been handed the task of producing your company's next blog post. Using the "three questions" discussed in this chapter, develop a topic of your own relevant to your industry and your audience that you can discuss in an educational way, with a twist you're not likely to find anywhere else. Remember to ask:

1. What does your audience need/want to hear about right now?
2. What's the right angle?
3. What's the punchline?

PART THREE
LEARNING

It's when we stop talking that we can learn the most about the person in front of us. It doesn't matter that screens and geography divide you from your audience. It's not a conversation unless they have a voice, too. If you listen carefully with humility, you give them agency to tell you how you can do better.

CHAPTER 8

Know When to Stop Talking

If you're a seasoned public speaker, you understand the value of "reading the room." You can sense whether people are actively engaged and taking notes or are whispering to their seatmates. As the speech continues, you might notice people drifting off or clicking on their phones, giving you the gnawing sense that you need to change your routine mid-stream to yank their attention back from their phones or whomever they're texting. Maybe you need to stop and let them ask questions. In a matter of seconds, you should be able to monitor faces and expressions, and have a plan for making adjustments in real time to reengage the audience when things aren't going well.

On a more one-to-one conversational level, think about the last party you attended. Perhaps you were chatting with someone you just met, talking about yourself or your family. Did the person seem interested? Did their eyes stay focused on yours? Or were they looking at their watch, or around the room hoping to escape? At some point, if you read the room right, you locked it up and stopped talking in order to gauge their interest. If you didn't, you'd never learn if they had any interest or where you needed to go next in the conversation to gain it.

The Importance of Reading the Room

Whether you're up at the podium or in the cocktail party conversation, you should be reading the room. In marketing-speak, it simply means monitoring peoples' engagement. In less polite language, it means "Shut up and listen!" Content marketing is a series of conversations you're having with your audience that are intended to elicit a meaningful response. Some approaches don't always work, and methods that once worked, stop working. Knowing when to stop talking is just as important as knowing what to say. It's the only way to truly get a sense of what your audience (or your potential customer) is thinking, and whether to stay the course in your strategy or tweak it. What are you listening for from your audience when you stop talking?

- What they're saying.
- What they're not saying.
- What needs to change.

Essentially, you're observing individual engagement. Is your story being shared and starting new conversations? Is the response positive? If so, what piqued the audience's interest and got them excited? If not, can you determine what caused the negative reaction? Unless you've done something egregious, bad news is often good news. A lack of response or a negative response allows you the opportunity to adjust and make changes to better meet your audience's needs. It's block and tackle until you make a touchdown. And as you learn, you get to know your audience more intimately, allowing you to reach them in more creative and effectual ways.

T3 Custom: A Case Study

At my own firm, T3 Custom, we learned the importance of taking a step back and listening early on. We started a monthly newsletter for a client aimed at an active investor audience, assuming the readership was pretty sophisticated, and as a result we could come out of the gate doing deep dives into complex investing and "aspirational" trading strategies. The newsletter delved into complex topics like futures, options, and foreign exchange trading, all the while sitting side-by-side with articles on investing, retirement, and personal finance.

We could have kept on pumping out aspirational articles on more complex topics, but after seeing what the audience engaged with the most each month—clicks on calls to action, number of reads, and time spend on each article—we heard a different tune. The articles that received the most attention were retirement-based investment strategies and "101" type trading articles, such as "How to Read a Stock Chart."

What were our choices? We could ignore the data and risk losing the audience or alter our strategy, bump up the retirement and personal finance articles, and reduce the number of complex trading articles. In time, the audience became more sophisticated and began "asking" for articles on those complex subjects. We were just too early. Our audience was learning and every month, we listened. As we tracked engagement, eventually, we went back to a similar mix with which we began.

Had we stuck with our original strategy, we would've alienated the audience out of the gate, and our young newsletter would have fizzled at a time we needed to raise awareness of our client's thought leadership, build trust in the brand, and grow the audience. The goal wasn't to force a certain type of content and hope the audience catches up. Our client had fallen behind their competition and had no SEO strategy. We helped turn things around by providing the content that was being asked for, finding unique angles to surprise and delight the audience, and at the same time, increasing the audience's level of sophistication and affinity for the brand. The only way we could've done this was by shutting up and listening!

●●

In any content marketing strategy, if you start off thinking you have all the answers, you're going to lose. Just like a human conversation, if you're always doing the talking, you're not listening. Are you hammering your products too much? Are you dominating the conversation? Have you derailed the conversation to a place where your customers are unlikely to follow? Stop and measure the impact of what you've been saying. Then think about how to read the results in a way that allows you to adjust your message and ultimately build a strategy that can bring customers through the door.

How to Monitor Engagement

Just as we covered qualitative and quantitative listening tools (in Chapter 6) before the conversation starts, the same two principles apply after the conversation starts. And both are equally important.

Quantitative: It's All in the Numbers

If a tree falls in the forest, but your data didn't track it, did it make a sound? So goes your content. Content marketing isn't marketing unless it's analyzed some way, somehow for engagement and, ultimately, ROI. But you don't need to be a rocket scientist and sift through mountains of data to understand if your content is working.

In a nutshell, these are the raw numbers of data that your content can be converted to. It's all about your audience and what they're listening to. For example, how many people are coming to your site? Which pages are they visiting? What's the daily volume of traffic your site is experiencing? By analyzing the data, you can better understand where to devote your resources in your content marketing as well as which resources are working and those that aren't.

Though there are many, a few are worthy of mentioning here, both free and paid options. First, let's look at the freebies.

Google Analytics

If you're not using Google Analytics, you're not really listening. I know I'll get grief for stating this, but you can't argue with the math. Google Analytics is the best free listening tool around and will give you as much or more information than many similar paid listening tools. You just have to understand how to use it—which isn't always easy. Google Analytics gives you incredibly valuable insights as to how many people are reading your content, how many came back, how long they stayed, where they went, where they're from, what devices they're using, and whether they clicked on any links.

Additionally, Google Analytics can track your audience without knowing names and dig in to see things including:

- Topics people come to your site to find but don't.
- A high-level overview of how well your paid advertising campaign drove traffic to your landing pages as well as how many of those visiting converted into leads.
- General demographic information, such as age, gender, interests, and geographic location about your landing-page visitors.

"Google Analytics can uncover deeper, more-actionable insights that can paint a clearer picture of the results your content is achieving now and reveal critical opportunities to make improvements—if you know how to track them down and analyze those insights," Jodi Harris of the Content Marketing Institute (CMI) notes.[1]

Other factors Google Analytics can help you track include social media traffic, blog post engagement, paths visitors take on your site, and whether people using mobile devices to access your materials are more or less engaged than people using other platforms.

And the truth is, Google Analytics does even more, more than could be listed here. And so, a word of advice: If you can only pick one listening tool to utilize, and you're just getting started, this is the one to choose and use.

Hootsuite (hootsuite.com)

Yup, this is a "before and after" tool for listening. Hootsuite features tools that help you monitor all your social media accounts in one place, alerting you to mentions so you can respond, and observe or join in the conversation. Social Mention collects data for you across multiple channels like YouTube, Twitter, and Facebook, and offers some entry-level analytics free.

Bitly (bitly.com)

This one is often overlooked as a listening tool, but there's more to Bitly than a simple gadget that helps you shorten link names. The company also provides real-time analytics, helping track clicks, increase engagement, and personalize customer experiences. If you have a lot of links and channels you're directing people to, Bitly might be a good resource to help you manage them and analyze which ones seem to be working best.

———

Other paid content analysis platforms, such as HubSpot, TrackMaven, Marketo, and Curata, all help identify which channels and campaigns deliver the most revenue and highest marketing return on investment. Although features may differ among them, all offer "Google Analytics on steroids" tools and reporting that can help you measure your progress and figure out what, if anything, you're doing in content marketing that's helping lead to actual sales. And when your content marketing strategy is mature enough and you've built an audience, you can more accurately assess ROI on certain pieces of content in the context of the whole campaign.

Of course, there are many more listening tools. This short list is to get you started on the variety available to you and what they're capable of helping you accomplish as you listen. Each of these, and in particular Google Analytics, is worth a look if you've reached the point at which it's time to step back and listen to what people are saying. After exploring these options, a simple Google search can help you find more and choose the ones that work best for you.

Now, although data is great for pinpointing trends and audience engagement, there's nothing quite like going directly to the source by having a *real* conversation with your audience to help you decide what they might want to listen to, and whether the data is off point.

Qualitative: Old-Fashioned Ideas Can Still Work

This is a deeper dive into engagement analysis, allowing you to ask yourself why people are engaging with your content and what they think of it. Qualitative research can also tell you what motivates the audience, helping you take a walk in your customers' shoes to see how your content resonates with them. Once you know this, you can fine-tune your strategy to target more specific customer groups and adjust your content to deliver what they truly seek.

You don't have to use the latest technology to stop and listen. The platforms mentioned above can help you dive deeper into the numbers, but they're not a replacement for good, old-fashioned "shoe leather" that, when combined, symbiotically produce the best results for truly homing in on what your customers are saying.

In the early years of advertising, "Mad Men" types in Madison Avenue high-rises who wanted to know what consumers were thinking convened focus groups. These live focus groups of consumers were gathered together and presented with survey questions in order to gather their thoughts on the company in question. Don't laugh. Some experts, even in today's web-focused content marketing industry, recommend interviewing customers either by phone or in person to get feedback. Some methods, unlike three-martini lunches, just don't go out of style. (Sorry, Don Draper.)

Post-Blog/Video Comments

Though you may not be ready to rent a room and hold a half-day seminar with your customers, you can use modern tools to get the equivalent information about them. This is the human side of engagement monitoring, more qualitative than quantitative. And it's two-sided, meaning you or someone at your company really must listen to what your customers say and be ready to act on it.

It's relatively easy to use any of the sites mentioned above to figure out where people are going on your site, how they got there, and what, if anything, they shared with others. But the questions remain: Why did they come in the first place, and what did they really think of what they found there? To analyze this, it's useful to have an actual person monitor all the interactions you get, especially the comment section of any social posts you've published.

Nearly every social media channel and blog has comments at some point. Once you build traction and have an audience, you should start getting feedback. People might respond with feedback saying, "Great article, but I have a question." Yes, they will actually start talking and having real conversations with you, and it's public because it's in the comments. You can respond to the comments or use the comments as a way to provide traction leading you to your next post.

If people are responding positively or even negatively in the comments, use those comments as a lead to understand what they're looking to see more of related to your content. If they have a question, perhaps you should use your next post to help answer it. If you start getting negative comments, try not to get defensive. Negative comments can be very helpful in course correcting your content strategy if many people feel negatively about something.

Surveys

When you want to know how people are truly responding to your content, just ask them. Just as you might survey your audience prior to creating content, you can ask them how you're doing and how they're engaging in them. Be sure to honor their time and apply the same rules of brevity as laid out in Chapter 5.

Surveys don't have to be long and cumbersome, nor do you have to send them independent of your blog. These days it's pretty simple to include short surveys at the bottom of your content asking readers for a bit of input. A simple question below an article asking if the page was helpful or not is an easy click for your customers and can provide a sense of whether you're delivering what they want and need.

Test It Elsewhere

You don't necessarily need to rely on comments on your own blog for a better sense of how people view your story. You can also offer to guest blog on a relevant sister site. For instance, I was a guest blogger on the Content Marketing Institute's blog several times. Because it's a heavily trafficked site, I gained invaluable feedback from comments posted after each contribution in real time. When one of the articles made the "top picks" for that year, I knew I was onto something.

If you're a guest blogger, you can post, see what sort of comments you get, and find out what people are interested in reading. In turn, that knowledge can help you learn about angles that might resonate on your own site with your own customers.

Again, we're using the example of content marketing, but other industries have similar educational arms. For instance, if you're a business leader, Forbes.com is an excellent platform that offers a chance to post opinion pieces to a wide audience. If your company makes generic medicine, perhaps you should check with the Generic Pharmaceutical Association to see what sort of content opportunities it might offer. If you run a coffee shop, there's the Specialty Coffee Association. The list goes on, and almost every industry has this sort of resource where you can test your message. Not all of them will accept a guest blog, but you can be sure there are conversations going on, and you can test your message as part of those conversations and gain great insight based on the response you receive.

The Human Touch

One more note about engagement monitoring: Don't forget to keep listening. It's easy to have a computer program like Google Analytics crunch your numbers and make a snap decision that you're on the right track. Then you go away and forget about it and a critical mistake is made.

That's not how to be successful. You need to revisit and reassess often, meaning someone in your organization must be responsible for this task. Ask yourself: "Has there been a human intervention?" Just because you got a certain number of hits or engagements doesn't mean it's working. What does the process mean, and what purpose is served? If you're trying to get people to a website, you can scientifically track that, but qualitative insight can be difficult to determine if you don't have an actual person thinking things through who understands the strategy at its core.

Going back to our opening metaphor, read the room. Take a step back and think about what the room is telling you. Are people engaged? Are they adding to the conversation? What if the feedback is bad? Schedule a regular meeting with your team to discuss the feedback you're getting, so you can take the time to consider what's behind the numbers and how to adjust your strategy. Just be careful of reading data in a vacuum.

Data Diving: What Can Go Wrong?

There's no doubt that data is critical to measure the success of your content. *But,* if you're not analyzing it correctly, or not reading the right data, you could be undermining effective content. This is where a lot of companies run into trouble.

Numbers come with their own set of problems, and as Albert Einstein said, "As far as the laws of mathematics refer to reality, they are not certain; and as far as they are certain, they do not refer to reality."

In other words, numbers are subject to interpretation. What you end up with might not reflect the true picture—something Einstein knew all too well. In the case of your content strategy data, this can be a potential struggle, especially if there's a rush among you and your colleagues to make the data correlate with preconceived notions or desires.

For one thing, there's likely going to be a lot of temptation—whether on your own part or among other leaders at your company—to interpret the data a certain way. Everyone is going to come at the results of the campaign with a different agenda, and you may feel pressured to make changes immediately that might not feel right.

But remember: Opening up and listening aren't just about stepping back and assessing your audience. It's also about being open to what the engagement data tells you, and not making split-second decisions, which might be based on some of the following mistakes. Here are four major pitfalls when it comes to reading data in a content marketing strategy.

Prodding the Data

The first mistake is one we just outlined, in which someone (perhaps you) looks at the data and tries to make it conform with preconceived notions. When data is used to validate an opinion, it's anticollaborative and can lead to biased decision-making.

How do you go about spotting the problem? Data from a single source, measured by one person, should throw up a caution flag. In cases like these, data might be getting measured without proper context, and/or prone to errors or omissions. Each of these scenarios should raise suspicion, with the possibility the person doing the analyzing is working in his or her own self-interest, rather than trying to come up with a broader assessment. Make sure this person isn't you, and also beware of others at your company who might take this approach. Be ready to argue your point and stand your ground.

Data Without Context

Carpenters are familiar with the expression "Measure twice; cut once." This also applies to content marketing strategy. Many companies measure once and then start cutting away like a first-grader with a new pair of scissors and a pile of colored construction paper. No pause. The thinking behind the action is "The data says X, so we need to do Y."

The problem is that hidden variables may be driving the results. Without collaborative interpretation of the data—such as allowing other members of the team, including yourself or your subject-matter experts—to challenge the insights, false assumptions can get made. You took the time to stop talking and listen to your customers. Good for you. Now stop and listen to the data being presented to you, and don't run off half-cocked.

Premature Data

Marketers sometimes make assumptions before a strategy can take hold and have an impact, which often leads to poor decisions. There is great pressure on marketers today to show immediate results, but you must try to set realistic expectations among stakeholders about how long it takes to see content marketing bear fruit. In most cases, data can be reasonably analyzed in six to twelve months, depending on the strategy and content channel. Prior to the passage of time, use your data analysis skills to make tweaks or identify early trouble spots. But don't make major changes based on the first batch of data. Building an audience who trusts you takes time because your content and your conversation needs to take hold.

Insufficient Data

If you have 100,000 people visiting your blog, and only three of them complain that the font size of the type in your blog is too small, chalk it up to macular degeneration of the three visitors. Your font size is fine. You'll never please everyone. (And when you increase your font size, someone else will complain it's too large.) Making changes based on small subsets of inconclusive data can lead you astray quickly and distract you from your true priorities. Don't be tempted by squeaky wheels. If a meaningful number of people complains about the same issue, then make changes.

Understanding the data you've measured requires multiple data sets, collaboration, and the ability to challenge assumptions. It also requires patience not to start chipping away at your strategy based on a few early data points. By taking your time and doing a careful analysis, you'll have a better sense that the correct assumptions are validated. Once validated, then you can take appropriate action.

The ROI Conundrum

After you've stopped, listened, and analyzed the data, your most important work might begin. Not everyone at your company—from the bottom to the C-suite—is going to understand how content marketing is supposed to work. It's likely you'll face questions about how to measure return on investment after you've conducted your research. Be prepared to discuss the long-term benefits, higher lifetime value of customers, and the lost opportunity costs as virtually all of your competition fills the content void without you. Remember: Content marketing generally sits on a path to purchase involving several touch points. Education is where the "prove it" crowd awaits your story. You don't want to get left behind by allowing your brilliant content marketing strategy to get hijacked.

———

Ultimately, a content marketing strategy must translate to ROI, but in most cases, this won't occur at the start. Though CMOs may tire of hearing the term, it's about audience and customer engagement. The more engaged an audience is, the more likely you will be able to convert the patience required to dollars. Your content marketing strategy is ultimately designed to bring customers and revenue to your door. You're not doing it for fun, nor to simply show off your social media prowess.

That said, it's very hard for a single content marketing effort (like an individual blog, post, or tweet) to result in the clang of a cash register. Again, we're not talking about putting up a billboard on Interstate 10 and watching to see how many more cars get off at the next exit to go to your restaurant. That's pretty easy to measure, and the results are pretty clear.

It's not that clean in content marketing. You're jumping into the middle of a bigger conversation and using micro-conversations with your unique approach. If you're new to the conversation, you won't be known. You have to build trust and not necessarily expect early ROI. Once you've had a legitimate run at your content marketing strategy and it's been out there six to twelve months, then go ahead and measure, and try to determine ROI. Just don't make the mistake of attempting to calculate it prior to that.

You might also have to educate your team to understand that just because you didn't get a certain number of hits or engagements doesn't mean your campaign isn't working. Remember that it's very difficult to track what ultimately led a customer to press the proverbial "buy" button. They may have been part of a conversation you participated in months ago and then moved along to other interests. But at some point, they saw a call to action of some sort and because of the work you did earlier, you're top of mind for them again and they go to your website.

If that sign-up doesn't happen for a month after they read your content, it's going to be hard to know if your blog post was the reason. A lot of marketers will measure ROI solely on the last click. Maybe there was an online banner with an offer and you can say they bought from you because of that banner. However, that doesn't take into account all the trust you built a month or two earlier when the customer was on your blog.

This attribution problem is a threat to content marketing because so many people make the mistake of expecting ROI right away, and, understandably, CMOs are increasingly under pressure to show ROI with everything they do. But it's not that simple. The truth is, if you're not using a content marketing strategy because it's hard to measure ROI, you may not be seeing the bigger picture. Content is king now, and it's not going away. And though there may be a lot of it, you have an opportunity to stand out because brands are still shouting. People want to have a conversation. They want to spend more time getting to know you, and like you as well. That's what content marketing is about—engaging over time, building trust, listening to feedback, and eventually having the customer see you as a partner. At the end of the day, it's about building an audience, not breeding customers.

Icebreaker

Using your fresh new brand personality (voice and tone from Chapter 1), think of three survey questions to test in a small sample of readers. Think about one main primary objective you're aiming for.

Think about what you're trying to get the audience to do and what you think they need to hear. I'll give you a hint: One of the questions should be a fill-in box asking for topic suggestions. Now you have only two to come up with on your own. Ready, go!

CHAPTER 9

Get Your Customer Involved

The Internet democratized the selling process, and today people are more interested and tuned in to what their peers and experts say about a product than the spin from a company's paid copywriters. Today's content is shared and consumed as a group, and much of what we like we is based on what others like—which leaves a big role to fill for "influencers" of any kind. The influencers can be your readers who comment, or the people who write the content.

There's now a two-way channel running twenty-four seven, and it's where your potential customers spend more and more time chatting with others and comparing notes about different products and experiences. There was a time when a consumer would hear about a brand or product through a tightly controlled media epicenter (i.e., TV, radio, newspapers, and magazines). Now there are dozens of channels, most of which are digital.

When was the last time you tried a new restaurant without reading about it on a blog, or reviewing it on Yelp or OpenTable? When was the last time you booked a vacation without reviewing where to go on TripAdvisor or an equivalent travel blog? You might have started with having seen something in an ad, but most likely you went further. And chances are, you read content posted from an "influencer"—either an authority on local cuisine and/or travel, or simply a friend, a friend of a friend, or a friend's friend of a friend on Facebook or Twitter.

Perhaps the influencer was a celebrity. As a society, we love doing activities famous people do—eating at the same restaurants, seeing the same movies, wearing the same styles. It's validating that we're a part of pop culture. Because famous names endorse products all the time in traditional advertising, it shouldn't be a shock that they might be getting paid to endorse products in the form of content through modern conversation channels, should it? Even if they're not being paid, sometimes all it takes is a celebrity being spotted at a restaurant where your friend snapped a photo and shared it on Snapchat or Twitter. When Mick Jagger of the Rolling Stones visited Chicago recently, the web flashed with photo after photo of Jagger dining and drinking at various establishments. It's logical to bet that many of those restaurants and bars got a bump in business in the following days.

Your company might not be selling cars or fine food, and Mick Jagger might never use your product, but it doesn't matter. In today's marketing environment, you'll need to tap into what others are saying and help make sure your potential customers see it to create a buzz. Seventy percent of consumers place peer recommendations and reviews above professionally written content.[1]

The two-way channel that's always playing means curating the conversation, involving your customer, and learning the art of finding and using influencers, whether they're customers, celebrities, or super fans who love your product. You've already spent a lot of time listening to potential customers and letting them speak. Now it's time to get your customers and respected industry influencers involved in telling your story.

How Much "Influence" Do You Have?

First, let's talk about the types of influencers you might want to tap into to talk about your company and product. Then we'll explore ways to get influencers to tell your story in more potent and creative ways. Identifying and getting in touch with influencers is just the start. Many companies are actively seeking out influencers to move their products and raise brand awareness.

Using influencers—or influencer marketing, as it's called—isn't a completely new concept or even something unique to content marketing. Arguably, it was influencer marketing back in 1910 when tobacco companies put cards with pictures of Major League Baseball players into their cigarette packages. (Sidenote: This offended non-smoking Pittsburgh Pirates shortstop Honus Wagner so much that his card was pulled, and most copies destroyed. Today, the remaining handful now often fetch $1 million or more at auction! Oh, the irony.)

Why did this work? After all, Wagner wasn't telling anyone how great the tobacco was that came along with his card. He just stared at you out of the package. The chance of getting his picture drew people in, kind of like customers who bought Willie Wonka's candy bars in hopes of getting a "golden ticket." Today, marketers have access to a host of influential people who can actually advocate for your brand, rather than just look cool in a photo, and companies are tapping into this concept—except it's not photos of themselves, but rather, their opinions.

Whether you use a celebrity or an industry expert, a 2017 survey by eMarketer.com found that nearly 90 percent of U.S. agency and brand marketers believe so-called "influence marketing" can positively impact how people feel about a brand.[2]

In the same survey, 70 percent of marketers said they "agree" or "strongly agree" that influencer marketing budgets will increase in 2018, which means only one thing: Even if you're not engaging in this tactic, your competitors probably are.[3]

Influencers are the people your potential customers may already be listening to simply because they're involved in the conversation, and you can harness their knowledge and reputation to help your brand. Sometimes they'll work for free, and other times they'll need to be paid (which, understandably, is met with greater skepticism). Often, just a little attention is all they're seeking. Ultimately, it comes down to who is curating the conversation—finding people with the right nuggets of knowledge that can be presented in places where the conversation is taking place and where potential customers are likely to see them.

Who Are the Influencers?

Let's explore a few of the key types of influencers that brands—both large and small—use today. There are three common varieties: external, internal, and paid.

External Influencers

An external influencer can be a blogger with a following, or an expert in the field, who is not getting paid to speak on behalf of your brand. Often, this type of influencer has something to say and is looking for exposure, and because they're also part of the twenty-four seven conversation already, so the people you want to influence are likely to "know" them.

The relationship with external influencers is symbiotic—a "you scratch my back, and I'll scratch yours." The scenario in which said backscratching is the tradeoff. Your influencer fills a content gap for you, and you provide them with exposure and more links to help their SEO, exposure, what have you. They get exposure to people interested in your mutual brands, and you get free content from respected subject-matter experts (SMEs). How does this work?

In my industry (content marketing, that is), there are a number of us who are all part of an early-to-market group who pioneered new ideas in content marketing before mobile proliferation and are often asked as influencers for content. We get invited to write blogs, speak at engagements, and get quoted frequently in various trade publications that focused on marketing.

Early on, Joe Pulizzi, shortly after creating the Content Marketing Institute, smartly realized giving his content away would be a great way to spread his (and CMI's) influence—thereby increasing brand awareness for his firm. After building a large following at content marketinginstitute.com, he created a video saying (I'm paraphrasing here), "Go ahead and take my content without asking. Just give CMI attribution!"

Though you're probably not trying to write a book or blog about content marketing, you do have a brand and a product, and there are well-known and respected names in your industry as well. Maybe you're already familiar with some of them. They're often people with recognized blogs or small companies of their own whom interested consumers seek out for advice. For instance, if your company sells musical instruments, it's likely that a number of recognized musicians have websites where people go for the latest advice on technique and gear. Observe which sites seem to get the most traffic, and which experts are quoted or referred to online and in hobby magazines. These are the people you should consider reaching out to as influencers.

Also, using an external expert to get your point across helps bring credibility. In effect, you're saying, "We're not afraid to admit we don't have all the answers, but we can reach out to someone else who might, even if they're not in our organization." It goes back in some ways to an earlier chapter when we talked about the importance of being humble. In essence, you're not just saying, "Take my word for it." You're bringing in a credible industry voice without a conflict of interest.

Internal Subject Matter Experts

Not everyone is going to have someone inside their organization who's already a big name in the industry, but if you do, it can be a huge advantage in getting noticed and becoming part of the conversation. An internal subject-matter expert is a free source of respect, which you should tap into as often as possible. There's really no limit.

When Steve Jobs and Steve Wozniak launched Apple—literally in a garage—the home computer industry barely existed. However, small computer clubs and magazines were out there, and both Jobs and especially Wozniak—who did most of the actual inventing—began attending club meetings and visiting computer fairs around the West Coast. Wozniak became a respected name among computer fans, and his reputation turned out to be a major advantage for Apple in getting its name out. In fact, it was Wozniak's demonstration of Apple's technology at a presentation to the Homebrew Computer Club in 1976, which helped lead to the company's first major order. According to Walter Isaacson's biography of Steve Jobs, the order came from a person who attended the meeting and went away impressed with Wozniak's circuit boards and microprocessor.[4]

Obviously, there was no such thing as "social media" the way we know it back in those days, but hobbyist clubs served a similar purpose, bringing people with the same interests together so they could interact and learn more. Wozniak and Jobs recognized this, and they also understood that trade media could help get the word out. A July 1976 article in *Interface*, a hobbyist magazine, explained that Jobs "communicates with many of the computer clubs to keep his finger on the heartbeat of this young industry." It quoted Jobs saying, "If we can rap about their needs, feelings, and motivations we can respond appropriately by giving them what they want."[5]

Today's hobbyist clubs and trade magazines are where your customers and potential customers hang out on the Internet, and now that you've found them, you can use your internal experts like Wozniak to help direct conversation.

When my firm, T3 Custom, launched an online monthly newsletter for one of our large financial service clients several years ago, we had built up a following of about 25,000 regular readers. One of the "market strategists" in the firm was a quasi-celebrity, who had appeared on financial networks regularly, including CNBC. Because he had built a media presence and a recognizable face, he had grown a healthy base of fans. Anytime he was featured in a company email and mentioned one of the articles linking back to our newsletter, our readership doubled that month. Every time.

When people perceive of an internal subject matter expert as a public authority, take advantage of it by getting them to contribute content or augment your existing content by linking to articles in which they're mentioned or quoted.

Paid Influencers

This one has a couple of caveats, first because it requires you to spend money, and second because it has a mixed reputation. In 2017, the Federal Trade Commission (FTC) began cracking down on influencer marketing in an effort to curb the practice of celebrities being paid to endorse products on social media without disclosing that they're being paid.[6]

But a paid influencer—like many YouTube stars who are asked to make appearances to give credibility and traffic—can have a big impact. If you write a left-wing political blog, for example, and you were lucky enough to have Barack Obama make an exclusive blog contribution and then tweet about it, you'd get a lot of interest. (At the time of this writing, Obama has 101 million followers.) Though I can't speak for Mr. Obama, big influencers know they're big, and they're not writing for altruistic reasons. They're doing it because they get paid.

KFC, a division of Yum! Brands, which admittedly has deeper pockets than most of us, enjoyed success creating YouTube videos featuring different celebrities dressing up as the famous Colonel Sanders of fried chicken fame. It's a creative campaign that's using social media channels to spark new interest in an old product—and revive an old icon.

Micro-Influencers

Micro-influencers are "everyday people with smaller but highly engaged social media fan bases," says NewsCred CEO Shafqat Islam. They give brands "an opportunity to connect with the most passionate members of their audiences. More 'regular' consumers, especially younger ones, will share their product experiences across their networks in ways which inspire trust. This user-generated content will continue to augment brand-generated content."[7]

The micro-influencer is also known as a "superfan" of your product and can wield a lot of influence. Typically, they aren't getting paid, but they have highly engaged social media fan bases and are more than happy to shamelessly boast about how great you or your product are, while giving you exposure to their base.

The super fan is a brand ambassador for you. For instance, consider someone who says, "I love McDonald's cheeseburgers." Probably a lot of people do. However, if this person had hundreds of thousands of social media followers, they might start writing about McDonald's cheeseburgers on their site. This could end up drawing people to the brand.

If you're lucky, you already have a couple of people you know about who are plugging your service or brand in the twenty-four seven conversation. And you don't have to be McDonald's to attract such "super fans." You might be surprised to know that even a company making one of the most mundane products you can imagine—butcher paper—found out it had a core audience of fans in an influential industry and took action to promote that fact.

••

Oren International: A Case Study

Selling "butcher paper" doesn't sound like a recipe for social media marketing success, but Oren International—a Florida-based paper firm—figured out how to leverage the micro-influencer model to scale up in, of all things, the booming barbeque industry.

It started when Oren president Alan NeSmith noticed a lot of orders for a certain type of pink butcher paper from Texas, the heart of barbecue country. After a bit of digging, he found out that Texas "barbecue masters" had discovered the pink paper was perfect for wrapping their meats, and thus in high demand.

According to NeSmith in his own blog, "Pink paper, also known as peach paper, has become synonymous with delicious Texas barbecue ever since Aaron Franklin began using it at his Austin restaurant, Franklin Barbecue, where people wait in line for upwards of six hours to sink their teeth into his world-famous smoked brisket."[8]

That's when the content marketing light bulb went off in NeSmith. He decided to spice up his marketing by promoting the paper to barbecue aficionados across the country, in part by letting customers and influencers speak online about the product.

This took the form of interviews the company conducted with several chefs and other barbecue experts in which these influencers attested to the value of pink paper, discussed why they used it, and talked about what made it better than alternatives. The company created a colorful spread for online distribution featuring the interviews, along with photos of delicious meats wrapped in the paper and ready for cooking, as well as a brisket recipe.

The company tweeted this to its followers, and also began retweeting posts from others in the barbecue industry, inserting itself in the conversation but using its influencers to tell the product's story to new audiences.

The experts Oren interviewed provided authentic, expert opinions on the product and what made it stand out. Because we already know that today's consumers don't want a top-down approach to marketing, this sort of influencer testimony fits right into the current rubric. For instance, Jeff Knoch, of Jeff's Texas Style BBQ, had this to say about the Oren pink paper:

"I see it continuing to grow because it's not just some fad gadget or experimental technique. As people try it, they find the premise is sound. It does exactly what we want it to do as pit masters. It's already become the standard for many restaurants and it's going to become even more popular with backyard chefs too."[9]

A testimony like that from a micro-influencer can be much more effective than anything a hired copywriter might say. Putting testimony from Knoch and other barbecue experts on its website was only the first step Oren took to involve influencers. NeSmith also reached out to self-proclaimed "hardcore" carnivore Jess Pryles, a cook, writer, TV personality, and respected authority on Texas barbecue, and had Pryles help spread the word. Pryles wrote about the company's pink paper on her blog, singing its praises.

"Folks around the world," she wrote, are getting "feverish over what is commonly referred to as 'peach paper.'"[10] She referred specifically to Oren and the demand for its product, noting its popularity and all the special requests the company was receiving.

This is a perfect example of influencer marketing at work. Oren found a person (Pryles) in its industry who's widely followed and respected, and worked to build a relationship and get her to attest to the product's value. Suddenly, it wasn't Oren itself telling potential customers about the merits of pink paper, it was Pryles, who spoke to her own base of fans.

The bottom line: All told, Oren saw a more than tenfold increase in pink butcher paper sales through its new blogging and influencer marketing strategy.[11] That's the power of conversational marketing.

• •

Employee Influencers

Don't confuse this category with internal SME influencers. It's not the same. But if you have a group of dedicated employees, you can ask them to help spread the word about your brand as part of a content marketing strategy.

A few years ago, newspapers found themselves struggling to stay relevant as the electronic world stole much of their thunder. Some newspapers came up with the idea of using their own reporters to generate attention online. The *Wall Street Journal* was an early exemplar. Starting soon after Facebook gained popularity about a decade ago, the *Wall Street Journal* had its reporters begin posting their own articles along with other articles from the newspaper on their personal Facebook pages. The articles were free, even for non-subscribers, and the idea was to bring a wider group of people to the paper's website. Their idea caught on quickly, and soon a number of reporters at many papers not only posted to Facebook, but also tweeted.

And today, they don't just tweet their articles. If you follow someone like *Washington Post* political columnist Jennifer Rubin or *New York Times* White House reporter Maggie Haberman on Twitter, you'll see they tweet multiple times a day about the latest Washington developments. Sometimes they provide direct links to their articles, but other times their tweets simply help get the word out about what they're seeing on their beats at that moment, without directly promoting their companies. Nevertheless, anyone who checks it out further will quickly learn whom they represent, resulting in extended publicity.

Generating Content from Fans and Customers

Getting an external influencer, internal SME influencer, or paid influencer to promote your product is relatively simple and can be as easy as reaching out and asking them for a short quote or an email interview, but the real creative flow comes when you tap into super-fans, employees, and customers to launch your brand into the twenty-four seven conversation. A lot of companies do this, and they continually come up with new ways to do so effectively.

As I said at the beginning of the chapter, this sort of two-way communication with customers and fans directing the flow and driving brand awareness is really what separates today's marketing from the bullhorn advertising of the past. These conversations may already be going on, and your job is to tap into them and direct them in ways that serve your goals.

Getting Customers Involved

What you want to consider doing is starting a "feedback loop," using social media to get the conversation going. A feedback loop means customers and others with interest in your brand start the conversation, and that spreads virally to other people and into other conversations. What are some ways to get a feedback loop going?

Monitor What Customers Say Online and Respond

One way to jump into the conversation is to see what your customers are saying and immediately respond. Take the story of a twenty-three-year-old fan of Shake Shack, whose adoration for Shake Shack prompted her to tweet her beloved hamburger fav with "And God said, 'Let there be Shake Shack. And He saw that it was good.'" The company responded, "Amen."

This type of conversation also falls under the category of molecular level relevancy. (See Chapter 5.) And yes, real-time customer service on Twitter definitely falls under the conversation category.

Millennial customers tend to spend a lot of time on social media and can get a real sense of connection when they're acknowledged on social media by a favorite brand. This sort of communication isn't too time consuming and can pay big dividends. Think, for instance, of how many other potential customers this person likely alerted to Shake Shack's retweet of her post.

The point is, brands need to engage, engage, engage in conversation. Any conversation qualifies as content today because everyone is watching. Always respond to what is being said by your customers. Don't risk looking lazy or uninterested and lose an opportunity to capitalize on free content. Have a person monitor social media posts and respond positively and graciously. Always.

Monitor Sales Trends:
There Might Be a Social Media Opportunity

Finding customers, listening to what they say, and responding is a reactive process. You're hearing them, learning what they care about and what they might want to change, and then acknowledging them in the same channels. A proactive step is to find out if there are any trends involving your brand and then taking advantage of the content marketing opportunities they might offer. This often means taking a deeper dive into your sales results, like Oren International did.

Take Advantage of User-Generated Content (UGC)

When your customers and experts praise your product on social media channels, you've already succeeded at directing the twenty-four seven conversation where you want it to go without showing too much of your own hand or risking a top-down approach. The next phase, and one that's growing in popularity across many industries, is having your customers actually generate your social media content—in other words, "user-generated content," or UGC.

Millions of words are written about millennials and their nearly constant presence on social media, but generation Z, born just after the millennials, might be even more tuned in to what's trending. This generation is arguably at the heart of a growing trend in which companies ask people to contribute their own marketing ideas—often in video form—and post them on social media sites such as YouTube.

Too often, today's youth gets chided for their focus on getting online recognition, something that might frustrate their parents. On the other hand, it's a natural human emotion, and user-generated content taps into people's inherent desire to be recognized and appreciated. When your brand shares something a customer or fan created, the external recognition not only strengthens the customer or fan's affinity with the brand, it encourages the person to share the content further with his or her friends (and your brand benefits vicariously).

Consider the example of sixteen-year-old Carter Wilkerson, who tweeted while at Wendy's asking how many retweets it would take to get a year of free chicken nuggets. Wendy's reply: 18 million. And while he hasn't hit the 18 million milestone just yet, the 3.62 million retweets of the Nevada high schooler's original tweet was good enough for Wendy's to give him twelve months of free nuggets.[12]

On April 1, 2017, Wilkerson had 138 followers. As of April 2018, it's more than 100,000, and #NuggsForCarter has a custom emoji featuring a box of Wendy's nuggets. He got some help along the way with retweets from other brands and celebrities getting in on the fun. And in addition to the year-long nuggfest, Wendy's also donated $100,000 in Wilkerson's name to the Dave Thomas Foundation for Adoption.

But you don't have to be a restaurant to take advantage of user-generated content. For instance, yoga clothier Lululemon's #TheSweatLife campaign, in which the company asked people to share images of them "getting their sweat on," resulted in 250,000 uses of the hashtag, more than 7,000 photo submissions through Twitter and Instagram, more than 40,000 unique visitors to the microsite created for the campaign, and a massive boost in conversions.[13]

UGC can get a bad rap because it's sometimes used as a shortcut to simply throw content up and check off the box. But when used thoughtfully and strategically, UGC can be extremely effective for generating traffic, engagement, and sales.

Encourage Sharing

When you look at the results of some of these efforts, it shows the power lying latent in your customer base. Remember at the end of the day, you're trying to make an emotional connection to an audience. They want to be educated, entertained, and delighted. If you can make an emotional connection, the audience members become your brand ambassadors and spreads your word for you—exactly what happened for the companies in the examples in this chapter.

You'll also notice the companies participating in this sort of user-generated content marketing encouraged people to spread the word. Lululemon, for example, asked its users to share their images on Twitter, not simply to send them to the company. It was the social media sharing that ultimately spelled success, and therein lies the lesson for content marketers. Encourage sharing. If the content isn't shared in social media, it won't go anywhere in social media.

How Do You Get Started?

There are some online communities where people already exert their influence, have a solid following, and can potentially spread the word about your brand. How can you get started on a path toward getting your customers involved? Some of the traditional sites like Facebook and LinkedIn can be helpful, but there are some newer ones you may not be familiar with include:

- *Klout (klout.com)*. This site measures multiple pieces of data from several social networks, and also real-world data from places like Bing and Wikipedia. It compiles a "Klout Score," a number between one and 100 representing a user's influence. The more influential the user, the higher his or her Klout score.

- *Mavrck (mavrck.co).* Mavrck allows users to identify and recruit validated, authentic influencers, advocates, referrers, and loyalists, while it tracks and analyzes posts and engagements. Basically, the site helps you find and tap into online influencers.

- *Revfluence (revfluence.com).* This platform has some of the same goals as Mavrck, helping people grow their brand's social media presence by harnessing online influencers and generating original content.

- *SheSpeaks. (shespeaks.com).* The goal of this online community is to help elevate and amplify women's voices. SheSpeaks members have the opportunity to voice their opinions on everything from how they live their lives to what products they choose and why. Members test and review products, weigh in on topics via surveys, discussion forums and polls, attend VIP events, and even get to star in the SheSpeaksTV videos.

Each of these platforms are worth exploring if you have questions about how to get an influencer marketing campaign off the ground. They do the heavy lifting and help you put all the right pieces in place for an influencer program if your resources are thin.

How Can You Measure Success?

If you build a strategy and get customers and influencers talking about your product, how then do you measure success? Return on investment is probably what your company's management and its investors (if you have them) want to see. Content marketing is tricky. Traditional marketers want instant results, meaning quantitative results, such as how many people read your content and how many purchased the product based on that content.

The goal is to get CMOs and marketing partners to buy into the process and ecosystem of a long-term content marketing plan—which means you have to be involved in a conversation that moves people over time. A content marketing campaign isn't a billboard on the highway, so engagement is critical. The goal is not to make a million dollars (though that would be nice). The goal should be a more realistic and engagement based, such as building an audience of 25,000 people.

At T3 Custom, we faced a situation where we were under pressure to prove the value of the print magazine we published for a brokerage client of our new company (another larger online brokerage firm) that was buying it. We were worried the newcomer wouldn't see the value of a printed magazine and would look to save money by scrapping it.

We embarked on a strategy to prove our worth, starting with a survey that every reader received. Because the magazine cleverly personified a beloved mascot of an irreverent monkey with a sophomoric sense of humor, we strategically placed a call to action in a widely read section of the magazine with the words "Save the monkey! If you don't respond, the monkey will get it!"

Fearing the magazine would get swallowed up and go away, the response from our loyal fans was amazing. More than 1,000 of the 30,000 readers responded, some with quips like "I would trade my spouse for a lifetime subscription."

The survey questions were designed to demonstrate the magazine's value. It asked readers if they'd ever made a trade as a result of our publication. (Seventy percent said yes.) The numbers spoke for themselves, and the suitor kept us and our magazine, because we helped them see the value.

Icebreaker

Put on your R&D hat and go find three blogs from main influencers in your industry. Spend some time on each one, skimming their content to get a sense of what makes them resonate with their audiences. What are they talking about and what is their unique angle? What do their headlines look like? How long are their articles? How often do they publish?

Try to get a sense for why they have a following and why they are considered subject matter experts. Would your audience benefit from their content? What would be a benefit to them if they plugged their content into your strategy?

CHAPTER 10

Ditch the Checklist

Before every takeoff, airline crews verbally work through an extensive checklist. There's a detailed set of tasks to cover before the plane can even push back from the gate, let alone barrel down the runway and lift its nose. The checklist provides a sense of comfort and security for everyone on board. The pilots know exactly what's been done and what remains to be done, and there's no nagging sense any critical factor was overlooked. Sometimes, air disasters are traced back to a crew neglecting to properly follow the safety checklist.

In business, we each have goals to check off as we build our brands and companies. Like pilots in the cockpit, building these goals and confirming they're accomplished makes us feel like we're on track, poised for a safe takeoff to securely cruise ahead. It is the reason books like this give readers a set of metrics, just like those you've seen over the last nine chapters. You've read tips for building content, entering the conversation, earning trust, taking a humble approach, and knowing when to step back and listen. You've dutifully marked off each of these steps and you feel ready to go out and launch your content marketing strategy, keeping your eye on the list, of course.

Some companies never go beyond this point. Like the airline pilots, they're happy to dutifully check off the requisite boxes and then turn on the autopilot. Maybe they'll implement changes if there's a bout of turbulence, but otherwise their content marketing strategy doesn't get much more attention. Does this work? For a few, maybe. There is often a sense of security from following the tried and true. Other times, the marketing team at these companies can't convince their higher-ups to attempt something new.

The problem with simply sticking to a checklist is your content marketing strategy will never evolve with the times, and you'll only be following the pack. To successfully navigate the journey and remain relevant, you'll need to consider factors a responsible airplane pilot and many less-inspiring companies would never attempt. Before starting, you need to ditch the checklist and take a step back.

And yes, this statement may sound odd. After all, the previous nine chapters emphasized building a checklist and ticking off every box. However, businesses that have built truly successful content marketing strategies over the last decade didn't get there by coloring within the lines. They asked bigger questions, about themselves and their companies' ultimate goals, and made sure their unique content marketing strategies aligned with a deeper motive than simply building profit or adding new clients.

Where Mission and Passion Intersect

At its core, a content marketing strategy can only succeed if you conduct a successful self-check and completely understand your philosophy. Every brand has its own personality and mission. Every effort you make after that needs to fit in with the particular angle you've developed, and your entire team needs to be on board. And finally: The mission needs to be a goal, task, or undertaking you feel passionate about and willing to stand by, wherever your business may take you. If you can find this mission, your content marketing strategy can all flow from it like a jet plane cruising along in front of a reliable tail wind.

We've talked a lot about the skill of "speaking human." This can be a learned trait, but it's also an introspective one. You can use it on your own before trying it out with others. Before reading further, take a moment and ask yourself: "What is my firm's passion? What do I want to do that's bigger than making money?" Your answers should be short and sweet, stated in terms that anyone can understand and that can be applied to any conversations you begin in a blog post or as part of an ongoing social media conversation. If you can't answer these questions, perhaps take a look back to Chapter 7 about starting the conversation and think about how you want to jump in. This might trigger some specific thoughts on your broader goals.

I started T3 Custom with the mission to simplify investor education through the lens of content marketing. Soon after launching our first product, we started getting calls from banks and financial advisory firms, asking for our help, but on deeper and deeper levels. Soon we evolved our mission to cover all financial services. We wanted to help make the universe of financial services safer by empowering everyone with information that was easy to digest, and far less intimidating than the high-brow language used by so many financial services firms. Everything we've done since then supports that mission.

What we did was humanize our strategy, and that's what you need to consider as well. Beyond SEO, customer engagement, and ROI, be sure you're doing what's right for your firm and your audience. Ditch your checklist and forget about what everyone else is doing. It has to be organic. And it has to be true to your particular mission, once you understand what that mission is.

Each content strategy has its own set of rules. Sure, there are templates to follow, like the ones presented here. But like a fingerprint, every plan is different and organic in some way. The way you engage your own audience will be different. And no two content marketing strategies will work exactly the same. The first nine chapters of this book gave you the template for how to have a conversation within your content marketing strategy. Now it's time to step back and make sure you're having the *right* conversations internally before you have the external conversations with your audience. Determine how your own company's mission fits into your content marketing strategy in a way which separates you from the pack.

Brands Digging Deep: Four Companies Going Beyond the Conversation

Let's look at four brands that wholeheartedly embraced conversation in a big way. No dipping their toes in the water here. Instead of following the herd, they placed big bets on strategies that were largely untested at the time of their inception, while ditching the tired old language that used to characterize traditional marketing. Each brand ditched the checklist; they understood their content mission, and they stuck to it. They zeroed in on exactly what their customers needed and their willingness to have a real conversation with them.

American Express

In 2007, American Express saw an opportunity to bring together important influencers to build an audience of small business owners (who all need loans and credit cards) to have a conversation together. Through a content marketing lens, they launched Open Forum, an online community of small business owners who help each other to share practice management tips and advice.

Although American Express's products aren't discussed in the articles themselves, its branding is all over the site. The community is peppered with influencer tips on everything from navigating international trade to reducing business expenses. The company set the bar very high by creating extremely helpful content that is also altruistic.

Marriott

Marriott has taken content marketing to a level of excellence few have been able to achieve, in part because they understand that content itself is as important to a marketing strategy as any advertising campaign. You may think of Marriott as simply a hotel chain, but they view themselves as more of a travel/lifestyle brand, and it shows in their massive commitment to content through storytelling.

When a company fully embraces the potential of content, there's no limit to what you can do. Marriott hires seasoned Hollywood names and leverages the utility and reach of YouTube and Instagram to brilliantly create and distribute some memorable and highly sharable content such as mini-feature films and web series. In 2015, they created a short film, *French Kiss*, which resulted in $500,000 in room bookings in just sixty days after its release.[1]

But it goes much further with Marriott. To get a sense of how deep they're going into content marketing, check out Marriott's Renaissance Hotel Navigator

program if you get a chance (renaissance-hotels.marriott
.com/navigators). The hotel has handpicked local
"navigators" in various cities who provide on-the-ground
expertise about their towns. People may think of a hotel
as a transient place to stay, but Marriott expertly paints
itself as a knowledgeable partner that can help you get
to know where to find the best street food around or a
decent live music venue. Online profiles of each city's
navigator add to the sense that you're in touch with a
local, caring person, not a big, soul-less corporation.
Excellent.

TD Ameritrade

TD Ameritrade is a big proponent of investor education
and was an early adopter of creating separate content
brands for its various initiatives to accommodate its wide
audiences of online, self-directed investors and traders.
Its branded content products range from a suite of
digital products to humorous technical manuals and
college trading courses, to print magazines, and most
recently, a live financial news media network called
TD Ameritrade Network.

Amongst these, TD Ameritrade publishes *The
Ticker Tape* (tickertape.tdameritrade.com). In addition
to daily market commentary (a reason to come back
daily), what *The Ticker Tape* does so well is find ways
each day to educate investors with timely, informative
articles across the spectrum and make it easy for each
type of investor to find their niche. If you want advice

on how to pay for college, it's there. If you want to execute an "iron condor" options trade, there's an article for you. Most of the content on *The Ticker Tape* is written by financial experts who themselves have been in the trenches. Putting all this together into one conversation-friendly platform and continually evolving it to accommodate the needs and desires of its loyal fan base speaks to a huge commitment by TD Ameritrade for both its clients and the public, setting an example for the entire financial services industry.

Red Bull

I'd be remiss if I didn't mention perhaps the world's most successful content brand—Red Bull Media. It's so huge, it's said the content brand itself makes more money than Red Bull's energy drink business does. Why? They know their audience cold, and they set out to create a media brand from the start. They target adrenaline-rushed, thrill-seeking adventurers who often participate in extreme sports and activities themselves. They never stray from their formula, and other than the token extremist gulping down a Red Bull on camera or the Red Bull logo slapped on the athlete's equipment, they never talk about their brand. Their thousands of videos are distributed and shared across a gamut of properties, including the *Red Bulletin* magazine, Red Bull TV, RedBull .com, Red Bull Mobile, and yes, even Red Bull Music.

Whether you're watching some extremists in wing suits BASE jumping and landing into a plane in midair

(4 million YouTube hits), Felix Baumgartner's record-breaking 128,000-foot freefall from outer space (43 million hits on YouTube), Red Bull Media knows exactly what its audience wants and wins every time. Their social media numbers alone are staggering:

- 47 million Facebook fans,
- 7 million YouTube subscribers,
- 2 million Twitter followers, and
- 2 million copies of *The Red Bulletin* magazine in circulation in eight countries.[2]

All of this added up to $2.9 billion in U.S. beverage sales—nearly twice as many as the nearest competitor.[3] You can't dismiss the power of visual storytelling via content marketing with numbers like this. I can't say enough about Red Bull's their commitment to their content brand, and their ability to have and hold the longest running conversation with their fan base and generate massive sales from their effort. It's one of the few brands where people actively seek out its content.

What Not to Do

When you put the checklist down, it's also important to look for what you might be doing wrong. In Chapter 7, we talked about some of the "wrong ways" to start a conversation. Taking a higher view, it's worth taking another gander at where there might be holes in your bigger content strategy before closing this particular conversation.

Casting Too Wide a Net

If done appropriately, casting your net can be a catch all for your entire audience. That means even if you have a wide spectrum of customers with different interests, they can all find what they need through your content marketing campaign. But if you stretch things too far and cast too wide a net, you risk alienating your key audience.

It goes back to the foundation of organizing the content on your website so it's completely relevant. Take the stock market for example, as subject matter. You have both long-term investors and short-term traders. Your site should be organized so your audience can home in on what interests them. Traders might get tired of sorting through a heavy dose of articles about long-term investing, especially if the trading articles fall off your page after just a couple of days or you go a week or two without posting new content. You have to organize the information on your site or blog so it's easy for customers to find the information they're looking for.

One of our clients had five demographics of people they wanted to reach: investors, savers, retirees, stock traders, and options traders. To do so, the client had to ensure none of the topics of interest were ever buried. The home page of the financial media site we created for them was a catch all for each demographic—a simple click away. Each category had its own landing page and was treated like its own blog, with relevant content just to that subject matter that our client could market a desired audience directly to, and bypass the homepage altogether.

You're Difficult to Find

If you don't have an organized editorial strategy—which is obvious if your website is confusing and difficult to navigate—then you'll alienate your audience. Once someone decides not to come back, that's it, you've lost your opportunity with them. You generally have only one chance to get people to your site or channel, and the first impression is what keeps them coming back. Making the content relevant and easy to find is critical when you have less than five seconds for someone to make up his or her mind!

You're Too Quiet

Make sure you're regularly serving up fresh, relevant content. You can't just throw up a blog and hope people come to read it. You have to be committed to frequent updates. Create a content (editorial) calendar and commit to set intervals in which you publish content. New content, updated regularly is paramount, along with making sure your content is relevant and useful.

What About the Naysayers?

Despite the numbers, there are still a few hangers-on who dismiss content marketing. I can only assume they have little experience with it, and if they did, the campaigns they've been a part of have broken some or all the rules of this book.

Though you can show them a number of examples, right from these pages, of companies who are fully invested in and successful with content marketing, it comes down to a few basic facts:

1. Content is your twenty-four seven conversation with a captive audience when you can't be there.

2. Content serves people and machines (your customers and search engines) in a game of "Duck, Duck, Goose" that you need to be a part of. You can't win if you don't play.

3. Content builds trust. Trust builds audiences. Audiences build businesses.

4. The opportunity costs of not having a conversation through content are greater than the investment in having one.

5. Millennials, Gen Z, and everyone born hereafter are more trusting of conversations through content than selling through advertising. You need both, but they are no longer mutually exclusive.

If it will help, forward my post from t3custom.com on this subject at bit.ly/t3custom_CMnaysayers.

Dale Carnegie's book *How to Win Friends and Influence People* was first published in 1935 and remains influential more than eight decades later. You can bet that content marketing is also going to have a long shelf life, because it pulls together many of the things we're about as humans: connection, curiosity, commerce, and of course, story.

Welcome to the Conversation Age.

AFTERWORD

The Last Word

It doesn't matter what industry you're a part of. In the Conversation Age, we're all publishers now. Let that sink in for a minute. You wouldn't sell a product or service that was just "good enough." Your content shouldn't be "good enough," either, because your content *is* your product. And the conversations you choose to have across the digital divide is part of your service. Traditional marketing strategies may continue to dominate for years to come, but few companies will thrive without a core content marketing strategy that complements the overarching marketing objectives.

At a time when everyone is competing with the same entry stakes (low prices, great service, etc.) and valued attributes (creative solutions, cutting edge technology, and the like), the differentiator today often comes down to content. And with that, how well your content takes care of the audience's information needs, assuages their fears, and solves their pain points will have a lot to do with your content marketing success.

Be patient, though. If you're just starting out with a new content marketing plan, it could take a while to see results. Cultivating long-term relationships with your audience is well worth the time and investment. The whole premise of content marketing is not instant gratification, but rather building stronger ROI over time with your customers. By ingratiating yourself to your audience, and earning their trust over time, you'll enjoy a greater lifetime value with each customer, along with a bigger halo effect as they share their experiences with others they bring into your world.

APPENDIX A

Rubber, Meet Road

Conversation marketing is not rocket science. But doing it well is a learned skill set. Here's a consolidated set of the most important tenets from this book to remind you of your content mission as you look to start your own conversations with your audience.

- Showcase your vulnerability to your customers and win their appreciation for your honesty. Conversations build long-term relationships, not cheap dates. Speak human with them, and they'll return the favor tenfold.

- It's not how loud you can shout with megaphones, slogans, or noise. The noise gets tuned out. Rather, be mindful of what you say and how you say it.

- There's only one person sitting on the other side of the screen from you. They might be meeting you for the first time. What do you want to say to them right now that will change their lives? Make your handshake moment with them count for something.

- Customers no longer grade you on a positive curve just because you're bigger than your competitor. Audiences today expect humility and respond less to "corporate-speak." They're looking to connect—even if you're selling toilet paper.

- Be approachable to your audience as you would if they knew you personally, so that it's easier for them to reach out to you when they need your help.

- Provide solutions for your audience's pain points, even if it doesn't involve your product. All good content strategies are built on trust. Trust is earned by focusing on the needs of others, not your own.

APPENDIX B

Putting It All Together

For those of you who want to skip right to it, the following is a master "cheat sheet" of all the major points covered in this book to get you going on having the right kind of conversation in your content marketing strategy. You may already know enough and want to home in on a specific place to learn more. If so, use this list as a tool to help locate the specific chapter addressing your question.

Before the Conversation: Know Your Audience

1. Decide how you want to start the conversation. (Chapter 7)
2. Listen. Use listening tools (mentioned in Chapter 5) to research keywords and subjects trending in search engines (SEO) to make the robots happy.

3. Using the rules of conversation covered in this book, produce useful, memorable, keyword-rich content. (Chapter 1)

4. Find your audience's "pain points." What problems are they experiencing that you can help solve? (Chapter 3, Chapter 7)

5. Go where your customers are congregating. Find out where they're gathering online and make sure you're also there. (Chapter 8)

6. Hire specialists to write and produce the content relevant to your audience. (Chapter 6)

7. Keep tabs on your audience's likes and dislikes in social media. (Introduction)

Start the Conversation: Seven Steps to a Great Piece of Content

1. Tie your content to your goal. (For instance, T3's goal was to inspire investors to trade more.) (Introduction)

2. Consider whom you're writing for (the personality of your audience, or "persona"). (Chapter 1)

3. Keep in mind the Four Cs: clear, clever, concise, consistent. (Chapter 1)

4. Answer "the only three questions you'll need to ask." (Chapter 7)

5. Craft a great headline for bots and humans. How will yours stand out? (Chapter 7)

6. Join the conversation and remember to be humble. (Chapter 2, Chapter 3)
7. Step back and listen. (Chapter 4, Chapter 8)

After the Conversation: Listen to Your Audience

1. Remember to "read the room" to make sure you're not talking too much and the audience is still paying attention. (Chapter 9)
2. Consider letting others speak who can tell your story from their own perspective. Learn about different types of influencers. (Chapter 9)
3. Learn how to "mirror" your audience so they know you can hear them. (Chapter 8)
4. Go beyond the screen. Consider hosting meetings or seminars that attract your audience. (Chapter 5, Chapter 8)
5. Look for your audience's questions and address them, either with answers or new posts. (Chapter 8)
6. Let your customers speak on your behalf. (Chapter 9)

The Power of Patience

1. Track quantitative data on your campaign, but don't put too much importance on the initial numbers. (Chapter 8)

2. Avoid the "ROI conundrum." Remember that content marketing doesn't promise immediate payoff in new customers and cash. (Chapter 8)

3. Don't expect instant hits. A content marketing campaign takes time. You're building trust with your audience, not selling them a product (at least not at first). (Chapter 8)

4. Learn ways to prove you're growing influence, even if it's not measured in sales. (Chapter 9)

5. Be relevant. Qualitatively "police" your quantitative findings with a human subject matter expert to determine what is relevant to make your readers happy. (Chapter 6, Chapter 8)

6. Be ready to educate your team about the need to step back and wait for ROI. Not everyone will be on board, and your job is to help convince them. (Chapter 8)

7. Learn how to build calendars and stick to them. (Chapter 4)

NOTES

Introduction

1. Stanley Bing, "The New ABCs of Business," *WSJ.com*, April 11, 2014, *www.wsj.com/articles/the-new-abcs-of-business-1397255723*.
2. "Digital Marketing: The What, Who, How and Why of Digital Marketing," eLink.io, September 19, 2017, *https://blog.elink.io/digital-marketing/*.
3. "Content Marketing Statistics and Trends—2017," point visible.com, *www.pointvisible.com/blog/content-marketing-statistics-and-trends-2017/*.
4. Laila Cabo, "Make Me Cry: The Story Behind Wrigley Gum & Haley Reinhart's Unforgettable 'Sarah & Juan' Ad," Billboard.com, October 21, 2015, *www.billboard.com/articles/videos/popular/6737465/wrigley-gum-haley-reinhart-cant-help-falling-in-love*.
5. Jacqueline Howard, "Americans Devote More than 10 Hours a Day to Screen Time, and Growing," CNN.com, July 29, 2016, *www.cnn.com/2016/06/30/health/americans-screen-time-nielsen/index.html*.
6. "Bring Your Challenges," Prudential.com, *http://corporate.prudential.com/bringyourchallenges/index.html* (accessed November 27, 2017).

Chapter 1

1. "2018 B2C Content Marketing Benchmarks, Budgets, and Trends—North America," Slideshare.net, December 5, 2017, *www.slideshare.net/CMI/2018-b2c-content-marketing-benchmarks-budgets-and-trends-north-america-83409149*.
2. "Digital Marketing."
3. Simon Sinek, *Start with Why: How Great Leaders Inspire Everyone to Take Action* (Penguin, 2011).

Chapter 2

1. "Mean," Wikipedia.org, *https://en.wikipedia.org/w/index.php?title=Mean&oldid=826604536* (accessed February 21, 2018).
2. Kevin Lund, "Markets Are Random, Your Portfolio Shouldn't Be," *tickertape.tdameritrade.com*, October 1, 2010, *https://tickertape.tdameritrade.com/thinkmoney/2010/10/random-markets-portfolios-76061*.
3. Seth Godin, "The Pleasure/Happiness Gap," *Seth's Blog*, October 2017, *http://sethgodin.typepad.com/seths_blog/2017/10/the-pleasurehappiness-gap.html*.
4. "Progress Is Everyone's Business," GoldmanSachs.com, December 28, 2017, *www.goldmansachs.com/who-we-are/progress/index.html*.
5. Eileen Sutton and Kevin Lund, "Why Your Brand Should Speak Human," ContentMarketingInstitute.com, November 2, 2014, *http://contentmarketinginstitute.com/2014/11/why-brand-speak-human/*.
6. David Vinjamuri, "Chipotle Scarecrow Makes Enemies to Win Customers," *The Huffington Post,* September 12, 2013, *www.huffingtonpost.com/2013/09/12/chipotle-scarecrow_n_3914281.html*.
7. "Top Social Media Campaigns from FMCG Companies: How Ariel's #ShareTheLoad Inspired Millions," Talkwalker.com, April 1, 2016, *www.talkwalker.com/blog/top-social-media-campaigns-from-fmcg-companies-how-ariels-sharetheload-inspired-millions*.

Chapter 4

1. "2018 B2C Content Marketing Benchmarks, Budgets, and Trends—North America." Slideshare.net,. December 5, 2017,

*www.slideshare.net/CMI/2018-b2c-content-marketing
-benchmarks-budgets-and-trends-north-america-83409149.*

2. Clare McDermott, "LEGO Shares Building Blocks for Social
   Media Content Fans Love," ContentMarketingInstitute.com,
   August 11, 2016, *http://contentmarketinginstitute.com/2016
   /08/lego-social-media-content/.*

3. Joe Pulizzi, "Build a Brand Content Empire: What You Can
   Learn from LEGO," ContentMarketingInstitute.com, June
   22, 2013, *http://contentmarketinginstitute.com/2013/06/
   build-brand-content-empire-learn-from-lego/.*

4. Ibid.

Chapter 5

1. Kevin Lund, "Three Ways to Screw Up a Good Article,"
   ContentMarketingInstitute.com, July 19, 2010, *http://
   contentmarketinginstitute.com/2010/07/three-ways-to
   -screw-up-a-good-article/.*

2. Mike Norton, The "Smell Like a Man, Man" Campaign,
   PG.com, 2010, *www.pg.com/en_US/downloads/innovation
   /factsheet_OldSpice.pdf.*

3. "Case Study: Old Spice Response Campaign," Dandad.org,
   February 2010, *www.dandad.org/en/d-ad-old-spice-case
   -study-insights/.*

4. Norton, The "Smell Like a Man."

5. "Oreo's Super Bowl Tweet: 'You Can Still Dunk in the
   Dark,'" *The Huffington Post,* February 4, 2013, *www
   .huffingtonpost.com/2013/02/04/oreos-super-bowl-tweet
   -dunk-dark_n_2615333.html.*

6. Jennifer Rooney, "Behind the Scenes of Oreo's Real-Time
   Super Bowl Slam Dunk," Forbes.com, February 4, 2013,
   *www.forbes.com/sites/jenniferrooney/2013/02/04/behind
   -the-scenes-of-oreos-real-time-super-bowl-slam-dunk
   /#2abe96f92e66.*

Chapter 6

1. "The Power Is in Our Hands to #SpeakBeautiful and Change
   the Conversation in Social Media," Multivu.com, November
   19, 2015, *www.multivu.com/players/English/7447351
   -dove-twitter-speak-beautiful/.*

2. Nina Badahur, "Dove and Twitter Launch #SpeakBeautiful to Change the Way We Talk About Beauty Online," *The Huffington Post,* February 19, 2015, *www.huffingtonpost .com/2015/02/19/speakbeautiful-dove-social-media_n _6713960.html.*

3. "Dove and Twitter #SpeakBeautiful," ShortyAwards.com, n.d., *http://shortyawards.com/8th/dove-and-twitter -speakbeautiful-2.*

4. Kevin McSpadden, "You Now Have a Shorter Attention Span Than a Goldfish," Time.com, May 14, 2015, *http://time.com /3858309/attention-spans-goldfish/.*

5. Brent Chudoba, "How Much Time Are Respondents Willing to Spend on Your Survey?" SurveyMonkey.com, *www.survey monkey.com/curiosity/survey_completion_times/* (accessed March 22, 2018).

6. Ibid.

7. Chunka Mui. "Five Dangerous Lessons to Learn From Steve Jobs," Forbes.com, October 17, 2011, *www.forbes.com/sites /chunkamui/2011/10/17/five-dangerous-lessons-to-learn -from-steve-jobs/#44e374103a95.*

Chapter 7

1. "David Ogilvy's 7 Steps for Writing Copy that Sells," Kissmetrics blog, *https://blog.kissmetrics.com/david-ogilvy/* (accessed April 30, 2018).

2. Carl Friesen, "The 5 Types of Content that Grab Attention for the Best Content Marketing," ContentMarketingInstitute .com, December 12, 2011, *http://contentmarketinginstitute .com/2015/05/content-writing-tools-tips/.*

3. Rebecca Cullers, "Millions Are Thankful for This Feel-Good Bank Ad and Its Overly Generous ATMs," Adweek.com, August 24, 2014, *www.adweek.com/creativity/millions-are-thankful -feel-good-bank-ad-and-its-overly-generous-atms-159275/.*

4. Trâm Lê, "Case Study: Reward Customers Like TD Bank + Bonus: Reward Effective Ways," ThinkMarcus.com, May 30, 2016.

5. "Starbucks in Hot Water After Asking Irish Tweeters if They're Proud to be British," The Guardian, June 5, 2012, *www.theguardian.com/business/2012/jun/05 starbucks-british-tweet-irks-irish-followers*

6. Herbert Ross, dir., *Play it Again, Sam* (New York: Paramount Pictures, 1972).
7. Austin Carr. "The Inside Story of Starbucks's Race Together Campaign, No Foam" FastCompany.com, June 15, 2015, *www.fastcompany.com/3046890/the-inside-story-of -starbuckss-race-together-campaign-no-foam.*
8. "Starbucks Makes Jubilee Gaffe in Ireland," UPI.com, June 7, 2012, *www.upi.com/ Starbucks-makes-Jubilee-gaffe-in-Ireland/74731339042941/.*

Chapter 8

1. Jodi Harris, "Simple Tips for Sleuthing Your Site Performance Using Google Analytics," ContentMarketingInstitute.com, February 19, 2017, *http://contentmarketinginstitute.com /2017/02/performance-google-analytics/.*

Chapter 9

1. "10 Stats that Show Why User-Generated Content Works," DNMNews.com, October 16, 2015, *www.dmnews.com /content-marketing/10-stats-that-show-why-user-generated -content-works/article/444872/.*
2. Stephanie Wharton, "Many Marketers Plan to Up Their Investment in Influencer Marketing," eMarketer.com, March 2, 2018, *www.emarketer.com/content/marketers-put-their -trust-in-social-media-influencers.*
3. Ibid.
4. Walter Isaacson, *Steve Jobs: A Biography* (2011), p. 66.
5. R.S. Jones, "Comparing Apples and Oranges," *Interface Magazine,* July 1976.
6. James A. Martin. "7 Content Marketing Trends for 2018," CMSWire.com,| December 13, 2017, *www.cmswire.com /content-strategy/7-content-marketing-trends-for-2018/.*
7. James A. Martin, "7 Content Marketing Trends for 2018," CMW WiRE, December 13, 2017, *www.cmswire.com /content-strategy/7-content-marketing-trends-for-2018/.*
8. Alan NeSmith, "Competitive BBQ Is Heating Up with Peach Paper," OrenInternational.com, July 19, 2017, *www. .oren-intl.com/blog/competitive-bbq-is-heating-up-with -peach-paper.*

9. *The Bare Bones of BBQ: 4 BBQ Experts Reveal Their Secrets for Using Pink Butcher Paper,* Oren International (Pensacola, Fla.), *https://cdn2.hubspot.net/hubfs/166086 /PinkButcherPaper_Layout_Final_PDF.pdf?t= 1518702063632* (accessed April 30, 2018).
10. Jess Pryles, "What Is Peach Paper? A BBQ Trend Explained," JessPryles.com, *http://jesspryles.com/what-is-peach-paper-a -bbq-trend-explained/* (accessed March 23, 2018).
11. "Inbound Marketing Ties Blogging to the Bottom Line," SproutContent.com, *www.sproutcontent.com/case-study /oren-intl-2* (accessed March 23, 2018).
12. "Carter Got His Wendy's Nuggs and a Twitter World Record," FastCompany.com, May 9, 2017, *www.fast company.com/40419538/ carter-got-his-wendys-nuggs-and-a-twitter-world-record.*
13. Harald Merckel, "3 Tips for Creating a Social Strategy Fueled by User-Generated Content: Not Only Is UGC Much Cheaper to Implement, but it Is Also Much More Effective," Adweek.com, February 22, 2017, *www.adweek.com/digital /harald-merckel-guest-post-user-generated-content/.*

Chapter 10

1. Drew Neisser, "Why Marriott Is a Content Marketing Mecca," AdWeek.com, March 22, 2017, *http://adage.com /article/cmo-strategy/marriott-a-content-marketing -mecca/308365/.*
2. "The Red Bulletin," Wikipedia, *https://en.wikipedia.org /wiki/The_Red_Bulletin* (accessed March 27, 2018).
3. "Market Share of Leading Energy Drink Brands in the United States in 2017, Based on Dollar Sales," Staticia.com, *www.statista.com/statistics/306864/market-share-of -leading-energy-drink-brands-in-the-us-based-on-case -volume-sales/*

BIBLIOGRAPHY

"10 Stats That Show Why User-Generated Content Works," DNMNews.com, October 16, 2015, http://www.dmnews.com/content-marketing/10-stats-that-show-why-user-generated-content-works/article/444872/.

"2018 B2C Content Marketing Benchmarks, Budgets, and Trends—North America." Slideshare.net. December 5, 2017. https://www.slideshare.net/CMI/2018-b2c-content-marketing-benchmarks-budgets-and-trends-north-america-83409149.

Allen, Woody. *Play It Again, Sam.* Film. Directed by Herbert Ross. New York City: Paramount Pictures, 1972.

Bahadur, Nina. "Dove and Twitter Launch #SpeakBeautiful To Change the Way We Talk About Beauty Online." Huffpost.com. February 19, 2015. https://www.huffingtonpost.com/2015/02/19/speakbeautiful-dove-social-media_n_6713960.html.

Bing, Stanley. "The New ABCs of Business." *WSJ.com.* April 11, 2014. https://www.wsj.com/articles/the-new-abcs-of-business-1397255723.

"Bring Your Challenges," *Prudential.com.* Accessed November 27, 2017. http://corporate.prudential.com/bringyourchallenges/index.html.

Cabo, Laila, "Make Me Cry: The Story Behind Wrigley Gum & Haley Reinhart's Unforgettable 'Sarah & Juan' Ad." Billboard.com. October 21, 2015. https://www.billboard.com/articles/videos/popular/6737465/wrigley-gum-haley-reinhart-cant-help-falling-in-love.

Carr, Austin. "The Inside Story of Starbucks's Race Together Campaign, No Foam." FastCompany.com. June 15,

2015. https://www.fastcompany.com/3046890/the-inside
-story-of-starbuckss-race-together-campaign-no-foam.

"Carter Got His Wendy's Nuggs And A Twitter World Record."
FastCompany.com. May 9, 2017. https://www.fast
company.com/40419538/carter-got-his-wendys-nuggs
-and-a-twitter-world-record.

"Case Study: Old Spice Response Campaign." Dandad.org.
February 2010. https://www.dandad.org/en/d-ad-old
-spice-case-study-insights/.

Chudoba, Brent. "How Much Time Are Respondents Willing
to Spend on Your Survey?" SurveyMonkey.com. https://
www.surveymonkey.com/curiosity/survey_completion
_times/. Accessed on March 22, 2018.

"Content Marketing Statistics and Trends—2017."
pointvisible.com, https://www.pointvisible.com/blog/
content-marketing-statistics-and-trends-2017/ Accessed
on March 23, 2018.

Cullers, Rebecca. "Millions Are Thankful for This Feel-Good
Bank Ad and Its Overly Generous ATMs." Adweek.com.
August 24, 2014. http://www.adweek.com/creativity
/millions-are-thankful-feel-good-bank-ad-and-its-overly
-generous-atms-159275/.

"Digital Marketing: The What, Who, How and Why of
Digital Marketing." eLink.io. September 19,2017. https://
blog.elink.io/digital-marketing/.

"Dove and Twitter #SpeakBeautiful." ShortyAwards.com.
n.d. http://shortyawards.com/8th/dove-and-twitter-speak
beautiful-2.

Friesen, Carl. "The 5 Types of Content that Grab Attention for
the Best Content Marketing." ContentMarketingInstitute
.com. December 12, 2011. http://contentmarketing
institute.com/2015/05/content-writing-tools-tips/.

Godin, Seth. "The Pleasure/Happiness Gap." Seth's Blog. October
2017. http://sethgodin.typepad.com/seths_blog/2017/10/the
-pleasurehappiness-gap.html.

Harris, Jodi. "Editorial Calendar Tools and Templates." ContentMarketingInstitute.com. April 2, 2017. http://contentmarketinginstitute.com/2017/04/editorial-calendar-tools-templates/.

Harris, Jodi. "Simple Tips for Sleuthing Your Site Performance Using Google Analytics." ContentMarketingInstitute.com. February 19, 2017. http://contentmarketinginstitute.com/2017/02/performance-google-analytics/.

"How Life Insurance Can Help Provide Stability for Millennials." Farmers.com. https://www.farmers.com/inner-circle/life-events/why-millenials-should-have-life-insurance/. Accessed March 22, 2018.

Howard, Jacqueline. "Americans Devote More Than 10 Hours a Day to Screen Time and Growing." CNN.com. July 29, 2016. http://www.cnn.com/2016/06/30/health/americans-screen-time-nielsen/index.html.

"Inbound Marketing Ties Blogging to the Bottom Line." SproutContent.com. https://www.sproutcontent.com/case-study/oren-intl-2. Accessed March 23, 2018.

Isaacson, Walter. *Steve Jobs: A Biography.* (2011).

Jones, R.S. "Comparing Apples and Oranges." Interface Magazine. July 1976.

McDermott, Clare. "LEGO Shares Building Blocks for Social Media Content Fans Love." ContentMarketingInstitute.com. August 11, 2016. http://contentmarketinginstitute.com/2016/08/lego-social-media-content/.

Lund, Kevin. "Markets Are Random, Your Portfolio Shouldn't Be." *The TickerTape.* October 1, 2010. https://tickertape.tdameritrade.com/thinkmoney/2010/10/random-markets-portfolios-76061.

"Market Share of Leading Energy Drink Brands in the United States in 2017, Based on Dollar Sales," Staticia.com, https://www.statista.com/statistics/306864/market-share-of-leading-energy-drink-brands-in-the-us-based-on-case-volume-sales. (Accessed March 27, 2018).

Martin, James A. "7 Content Marketing Trends for 2018," CMSWire.com,| December 13, 2017, https://www.cmswire. com/content-strategy/7-content-marketing-trends -for-2018/.

McCoy, Julia. "9 Stats that Will Make You Want to Invest in Content Marketing." ContentMarketingInstitute .com, October 22, 2017, http://contentmarketinginstitute .com/2017/10/stats-invest-content-marketing/

McSpadden, Kevin. "You Now Have a Shorter Attention Span Than a Goldfish." Time.com. May 14, 2015. http:// time.com/3858309/attention-spans-goldfish/.

Merckel, Harald. "3 Tips for Creating a Social Strategy Fueled by User-Generated Content." Adweek.com. February 22, 2017. http://www.adweek.com/digital /harald-merckel-guest-post-user-generated-content/.

Mui, Chunka. "Five Dangerous Lessons to Learn from Steve Jobs." Forbes.com. October 17, 2011. https://www.forbes. com/sites/chunkamui/2011/10/17/five-dangerous-lessons -to-learn-from-steve-jobs/#44e374103a95.

Neisser, Drew. "Why Marriott Is a Content Marketing Mecca." AdWeek.com. March 22, 2017. http://adage .com/article/cmo-strategy/marriott-a-content-marketing -mecca/308365/

NeSmith, Alan. "Competitive BBQ Is Heating Up with Peach Paper." OrenInternational.com. July 19, 2017. http:// www.oren-intl.com/blog/competitive-bbq-is-heating-up -with-peach-paper.

Norton, Mike. The "Smell Like a Man, Man Campaign." PG.com. 2010. https://www.pg.com/en_US/downloads /innovation/factsheet_OldSpice.pdf.

Nudd, Tim. "Ad of the Day: Virgin America's 6-Hour Preroll Ad Is Creepy, Warholian and Sort of Brilliant Welcome to BLAH Airlines." AdWeek.com. October 15, 2014. http://www.adweek.com/brand-marketing /ad-day-virgin-americas-6-hour-preroll-ad-creepy -warholian-and-sort-brilliant-160775/.

"Oreo's Super Bowl Tweet: 'You Can Still Dunk in The Dark.'" HuffingtonPost.com. February 4, 2013. https://www.huffingtonpost.com/2013/02/04/oreos-super-bowl-tweet-dunk-dark_n_2615333.html.

Pryles, Jess. "What Is Peach Paper? A BBQ Trend Explained." JessPryles.com. http://jesspryles.com/what-is-peach-paper-a-bbq-trend-explained/. Accessed March 23, 2018.

Pulizzi, Joe. "Build a Brand Content Empire: What You Can Learn From LEGO." ContentMarketing Institute.com. June 22, 2013. http://contentmarketing institute.com/2013/06/build-brand-content-empire-learn-from-lego/.

Pulizzi, Joe. "See What Content Marketing Success Truly Looks," ContentMarketingInstitute.com. September 9, 2016. http://contentmarketinginstitute.com/2016/09/content-marketing-success-awards/.

Rooney, Jennifer. "Behind the Scenes of Oreo's Real-Time Super Bowl Slam Dunk." Forbes.com. February 4, 2013. https://www.forbes.com/sites/jenniferrooney/2013/02/04/behind-the-scenes-of-oreos-real-time-super-bowl-slam-dunk/#2abe96f92e66.

Sinek, Simon. *Start with Why: How Great Leaders Inspire Everyone to Take Action*. Penguin, 2011.

"Starbucks Makes Jubilee Gaffe in Ireland." UPI.com. June 7, 2012. https://www.upi.com/Starbucks-makes-Jubilee-gaffe-in-Ireland/74731339042941/.

Sutton, Eileen, and Kevin Lund. "Why Your Brand Should Speak Human." ContentMarketingInstitute.com. November 2, 2014. http://contentmarketinginstitute.com/2014/11/why-brand-speak-human/.

"The Power Is in Our Hands To #SpeakBeautiful and Change the Conversation in Social Media." Multivu.com. November 19, 2015. http://www.multivu.com/players/English/7447351-dove-twitter-speak-beautiful/.

Trâm Lê. "Case Study: Reward Customers Like Td Bank + Bonus: Reward Effective Ways." ThinkMarcus.com. May 30, 2016.

Wharton, Stephanie. "Many Marketers Plan to Up Their Investment in Influencer Marketing." eMarketer.com. March 2, 2018. https://www.emarketer.com/content/marketers-put-their-trust-in-social-media-influencers.

"Mean." *Wikipedia.* https://en.wikipedia.org/w/index.php?title=Mean&oldid=826604536. (Accessed February 21, 2018).

The Red Bulletin. Wikipedia. https://en.wikipedia.org/wiki/The_Red_Bulletin (accessed March 27, 2018).

INDEX

ABOUT THE AUTHOR

Kevin Lund is a leading financial services content strategist and marketer. Since 1999, global financial brands such as TD Ameritrade, HSBC, Forbes, and Nasdaq have relied on Lund to develop content strategies bridging their marketing needs with their customers' information needs through thoughtful and intentional conversation. Through his work, he has developed digital and print publication strategies, branded education curriculums, and helped create customer-experience divisions. He has witnessed how these services can transform a brand's client service through clarity and consistency to create a high ROI. Lund's straightforward recipe of blending eye-level editorial and stunning visual design has earned his publications some of content marketing's top honors and industry recognition.

A veteran content marketer and strategist, Lund has helped leading global brands tell their story through a plain-English, conversational approach using digital and print media, including web, mobile applications, newsletters, magazines, live events, webinars, and more.

As founder and CEO of T3 Custom, Lund pursues the critical "kaboom factor" where story and content marketing intersect. Lund, whose firm has been recognized for its contributions and innovations in the content marketing revolution now underway, helps clients engage with their customers in meaningful, human ways that amplify ROI and thought leadership.

Lund is also recognized as an advisor/consultant for the Content Marketing Institute from 2010 through 2014 as well as director of education of the Optionetics division of Charles Schwab from January 2001 through February of 2007. In 2000, he created the live messaging platform for online options traders, which provided trade ideas and commentary in real time.

You can find Kevin on Twitter @KLundT3.